Academic Employment and Retrenchment:
Judicial Review and Administrative Action

by Robert M. Hendrickson and Barbara A. Lee

ASHE-ERIC Higher Education Research Report No. 8, 1983

Prepared by

 Clearinghouse on Higher Education
The George Washington University

Published by

Association for the Study of Higher Education

Jonathan D. Fife,
Series Editor

Cite as:
Hendrickson, Robert M., and Lee, Barbara A. *Academic Employment and Retrenchment: Judicial Review and Administrative Action.* ASHE-ERIC Higher Education Research Report No. 8. Washington, D.C.: Association for the Study of Higher Education, 1983.

The ERIC Clearinghouse on Higher Education invites individuals to submit proposals for writing monographs for the Higher Education Research Report series. Proposals must include:
1. A detailed manuscript proposal of not more than five pages.
2. A 75-word summary to be used by several review committees for the initial screening and rating of each proposal.
3. A vita.
4. A writing sample.

ISSN 0737-1292
ISBN 0-913317-07-1

ERIC **Clearinghouse on Higher Education**
The George Washington University
One Dupont Circle, Suite 630
Washington, D.C. 20036

Association for the Study of Higher Education
One Dupont Circle, Suite 630
Washington, D.C. 20036

This publication was partially prepared with funding from the National Institute of Education, U.S. Department of Education, under contract no. 400-82-0011. The opinions expressed in this report do not necessarily reflect the positions or policies of NIE or the Department.

John Lombardi
Consultant

Richard Lonsdale
Professor of Educational Administration
New York University

Linda Koch Lorimer
Associate General Counsel
Yale University

Virginia B. Nordby
Director
Affirmative Action Programs
University of Michigan

Eugene Oliver
Director, University Office of School & College Relations
University of Illinois—Champaign

Harold Orlans
Lawyer

Marianne Phelps
Assistant Provost for Affirmative Action
The George Washington University

Gary K. Probst
Professor of Reading
Prince Georges Community College

Cliff Sjogren
Director of Admissions
University of Michigan

Robert A. Scott
Director of Academic Affairs
State of Indiana Commission for Higher Education

Al Smith
Assistant Director of the Institute of Higher Education &
    Professor of Instructional Leadership & Support
University of Florida

ACKNOWLEDGMENTS

The authors would like to thank David Leslie for his thoughtful review of the manuscript and Eileen Trainer for her assistance with some of the research. Monique Weston Clague's technical assistance on several key issues was also much appreciated.

CONTENTS

FOREWORD

In 1978 the ERIC Clearinghouse on Higher Education
addressed the issue of faculty employment in a Research
Report by Marjorie C. Mix entitled *Tenure and Termination
in Financial Exigency*. Since that time the issues concerning
academic employment have grown more complex. Financial
conditions have not improved appreciably for most institutions and have deteriorated at many. Several issues have
increasingly complicated academic employment:

- The extension of the mandatory retirement age to 70
  years,
- the stagnation of faculty due to policies limiting the
  percentage of tenured faculty per academic program,
- a trend to supplement full-time faculty with larger
  numbers of low-paid part-time faculty, and
- a heightened pressure to develop liberal sabbatical
  policies in some departments but not others.

Although the courts have generally upheld administrative policies and procedures concerning academic employment, in those areas where they have not, the financial
penalities have been most severe. In this Research Report
by Robert M. Hendrickson, Associate Professor in the
Center for the Study of Higher Education at the University
of Virginia, and Barbara A. Lee, Assistant Professor in the
Department of Educational Administration, Supervision,
and Adult Education at Rutgers University, the major legal
considerations pertaining to academic employment are
carefully examined. This report written for non-lawyers is
designed to give the people directly involved with academic employment, (i.e., college and university administrators and faculty) a clear understanding of the issues
involved with faculty employment, as well as an understanding of how the courts have handled them. After a
thorough review of such employment areas as discrimination, equal pay, and financial exigency, the authors have
developed suggested guidelines for evaluating current
institutional academic employment practices. Colleges and
university decisionmakers will find this Research Report
extremely useful in (1) examining current academic employment practices and (2) developing procedures to help

minimize the need to use valuable institutional resources in academic employment litigation.

Jonathan D. Fife
Director and Series Editor
ERIC Clearinghouse on Higher Education
The George Washington University

EXECUTIVE SUMMARY

The 1980s will be an austere period for higher education. The current recession, chronic high unemployment, declining enrollment, decreasing or static federal support, and reductions in state revenues will serve to perpetuate the demand to reduce programs and faculty throughout the decade. As administrators plan for reductions and the elimination of programs, they need to be aware of developments in faculty rights and employment practices. These rights and practices include the legal issues of financial exigencies and the Age Discrimination Act of 1967 as amended in 1978, Title VII of the Civil Rights Act of 1964 as amended by the Education Amendments of 1972, Title IX and employment, and the Equal Pay Act of 1963. Knowledge of each of these areas and the rapidly developing case law surrounding them is important information for administrators in higher education.

[C]ourts have rarely ruled against faculty peer determinations. . . .

Areas of Judicial Deference and Scrutiny

An examination of the last decade of litigation over faculty employment disputes makes it clear that, although the potential for judicial intervention in academic decision making is undeniable, such intervention has occurred infrequently. Despite the courts' willingness to review peer evaluations in cases where faculty have alleged discrimination by a college, courts have rarely ruled against faculty peer determinations; when they have done so, the plaintiff has built a strong case of the evaluator's misconduct. Courts have upheld the right of faculty to select their own colleagues, to determine the curricular and research missions of their departments, and to evaluate their peers within and without their institutions. In particular, courts have upheld the right of administrators to curtail or eliminate academic programs, lay off tenured faculty, and establish standards for faculty members' conduct and performance.

Title VII of the Civil Rights Act of 1964

Judicial review of academic employment decisions challenged under Title VII or under 42 U.S.C. §1981 is becoming more predictable. Courts are more inclined now than in the past to examine the fairness and consistency of the procedures used to make employment decisions and to examine decision making for evidence of bad faith, arbitrariness, or caprice. But judicial review generally goes no farther.

Courts generally regard the substantive evaluation of a faculty member's qualifications, especially when conducted by the faculty member's peers, as presumptively valid, absent overwhelming evidence of misconduct. When the privilege of academic freedom is added to the substantial deference shown by the courts to academic judgments, it appears likely that an employment decision made in compliance with institutional policies, due process (if applicable), and disciplinary norms would be nearly impervious to challenge unless the plaintiff has clear evidence of bias.

The Equal Pay Act

Despite the fact that both Title VII and the Equal Pay Act are very specific in the burdens of proof required of both parties and the extent of the remedies available, the courts' approach in the various cases has varied widely. Clearly, some of the differences in the scope of judicial review may be related to variations in the ways plaintiffs presented their cases and the evidence plaintiffs relied upon. Much of the difference among these cases, however, appears to be attributable to the courts' individual views toward the appropriate judicial scope of review. This situation is unfortunate because it makes it difficult for both plaintiffs and defendant colleges to plan a strategy for litigation or to predict which claims may be most successful.

Such individuality in judicial approach is also evident when the range of remedies ordered in academic salary discrimination cases is analyzed. Remedies have ranged from salary adjustments for individual litigants to negotiated salary settlements for the institution. This uncertainty in remedies is especially troublesome to administrators who may be faced with the decision of settling or proceeding with the litigation. It would seem that administrators lose either way: Litigation is costly and damages in class action suits could be in the millions of dollars, while some attempts to ameliorate prior salary discrimination can actually engender litigation.

The cases, however, do suggest an approach to salary determinations that would not only aid colleges in defending lawsuits but could also lead to fairer salary decisions in the bargain. Heading an academic program, organizing service activities for a department, serving on important and time-consuming governance committees, among other activities, can serve as valid criteria for differentiating salaries. A valid merit pay system (based upon clearly articulated criteria) exempts salary determinations from the Equal Pay Act in that it justifies disparate salaries. Accurate and complete data on the market value of individuals with degrees in certain disciplines may justify discrepancies in the salaries paid to various otherwise "comparable" faculty members. Therefore, the courts have said, any salary distinctions among faculty must be carefully documented.

Title IX of the 1972 Education Amendments

It is clear, since the Supreme Court's ruling in *North Haven*, that Title IX covers employment. The Supreme Court will soon decide, in *Grove City*, the definitions of "program" and "recipient" of federal financial support. *Grove City* will determine whether indirect federal financial aid in the form of student loans and grants makes the entire institution a "recipient," therefore bringing the institution as a whole within the proscriptions of Title IX. Whether the courts take the broad approach or the narrow approach of using only direct federal financial aid in defining a program has serious implications for enforcement of the prohibitions of Title IX and future litigation against colleges and universities. A review of the specific regulations is useful for administrators with programs receiving federal financial assistance.

Financial exigencies and the Age Discrimination in Employment Act

Postsecondary institutions facing budget reductions may rely on financial exigencies as a way to reduce staff. The courts have certified financial exigencies as a valid rationale for removing tenured faculty. The institution, however, has the burden of proving that the financial exigency exists and that it acted reasonably. Requirements for due process in public institutions necessitate a written statement of the basis for the decision, a description of the manner used in making the decision, disclosure of information and data used in the decision making process, and an opportunity for the dismissed faculty member to respond. Institutions will find that possible litigation can be reduced by making a good faith effort to find other positions within the institution or system for those laid off as a result of financial exigency. Such an effort will also assist the institution in a successful defense in litigation. One court also seems to indicate that a breach of a contract, negotiated for a specific period, during that period would not be allowed for reasons of financial exigency.

The Age Discrimination in Employment Act will affect those institutions relying on retirements to reduce staff. Institutions must plan for the mandatory retirement age, under the act, at 70. As the Supreme Court and Congress are both reviewing the act, the requirements are in a state of flux. Administrators may want to make contingency plans based on the possible changes—for example, adjusting for a mandatory retirement age of 70, with the understanding that in 15 years there might be no mandatory retirement age. If public higher education is exempt from the law by a Supreme Court ruling, then contingency plans might include use of the institution's current mandatory retirement age.

Suggestions for Administrators

The following administrative actions are suggested as ways to help college and university administrators understand the purposes of the laws and how the courts interpret them for academic institutions.

- Colleges need to be able to justify the employment decisions they reach by clear data and careful documentation. Peer review *criteria* may vary by discipline, but the *procedures* for review should be consistent and applied evenhandedly.
- Faculty should be included in academic employment decisions because their inclusion results in better informed decisions, enhances employee relations, and may make the decision less susceptible to reversal by a court.
- Documentation at each level of the decision making process leads to greater accountability and more adequate explanation of the decision.

- At the time new faculty are hired, administrators should clearly identify the criteria that will be used in tenure decisions, should notify faculty how those criteria will be weighted, and should develop an annual evaluation process for all faculty.
- Salary increases should be based on documentation. Current salaries can be reviewed using regression analysis.
- The search committee's composition is not mandated by the laws, but it should not be limited to either sex or one race.
- The search committee's criteria for selecting an employee should conform to the job description for the position.
- Fringe benefits should be analyzed to make sure they are based solely upon nondiscriminatory considerations, not gender or age.
- Early retirement incentives should be developed to cope with the requirements under the Age Discrimination in Employment Act.
- In the termination of faculty for financial exigency, due process as prescribed by the courts should be followed. The decision of whom to terminate should be based solely on financial exigency; termination should not be used as a pretext to rid the institution of a "difficult" faculty member.

Administrators and their counsel can learn from the experience of their colleagues, and this report has distilled those experiences into approaches that can be generalized to employment practices.

ADMINISTRATIVE PRACTICES AND FACULTY EMPLOYMENT IN THE 1980s

Employment decisions in academe are seldom easily made, even in the best of economic times. Evaluations of faculty members' competence are of necessity subjective and frequently based upon ill-defined criteria. The myriad state and federal laws and regulations protecting employees from arbitrary or discriminatory treatment also complicate, and often lengthen, the process of making employment decisions.

But these are not the best of economic times. News reports about higher education have been replete with examples of institutional stress reflecting the current economic malaise. Near the end of 1982, the University of Washington was planning to eliminate 24 degree programs (Mitzman 1982). At about the same time, a panel at Colorado State University proposed program cuts and changes in tenure contracts from lifetime to a specific number of years (*Chronicle* 1982d). Northern Michigan University laid off 19 tenured faculty (Scully 1982), and a faculty organization contested in court Michigan State University's plan to reduce budgets through a layoff of all faculty for two days (*Higher Education Daily* 1982). News from the higher education community indicates budget cutting, layoffs, and program reductions. Clearly these actions are largely a result of the current recession. But even after this recession bottoms out, other factors—shifting enrollment patterns, declining federal influence and support, reduced state revenues, competition with other state agencies for revenues, current faculties' retirement patterns—could mean continuing reductions in staffing and programs throughout the decade.

Projections of enrollment suggest that program cutbacks will continue throughout the decade. "The most dramatic feature of the next 20 years, as far as we now know, is the prospect of declining enrollments after more than three centuries of fairly steady increase" (Carnegie Council 1980, p. 32). While enrollment recently increased 1 percent, the increase was limited to particular regions and institutional types (MaGarnell 1982). In part, it can be accounted for through increases in part-time and adult students; enrollment at community colleges continues to increase (MaGarnell 1982). Some colleges and universities, however, are capping or reducing enrollment to accommodate declining state funding. Within institutions, shifting

Projections of enrollment suggest that program cutbacks will continue throughout the decade.

enrollment affects specific programs. While demand may be high for engineering or business courses, for example, reduced enrollments are continuing in the humanities and education. When faculty positions are static or subject to reduction because of austere financial conditions or declining enrollment, the result is a shifting of faculty positions among departments and schools to adjust to different demands—or faculty layoffs.

Even at colleges and universities where faculty have not actually been laid off, new practices show the effect of the fiscal crunch. Faculty members' mobility has been reduced because fewer faculty positions are being filled. Many colleges and universities have made it more difficult for faculty to gain tenure by insisting on a higher level of publication or scholarship than was previously required. Other institutions have set quotas to stabilize the proportion of tenured and nontenured faculty. When full-time tenured faculty resign or retire, some institutions, if they replace them at all, are replacing them with part-time or visiting faculty or are offering only term contracts instead of tenure-accruing positions.

Despite the urgency of the continuing fiscal crisis and the need to cut back programs or staff or modify practices rapidly, administrators may not ignore the many legal protections afforded faculty. The award of tenure still bestows a property right upon faculty that must be respected even in cases of financial exigency. Laws forbidding discrimination against age, sex, and race in decisions related to hiring, promotion, salary, and retirement must be obeyed, despite the presence of a fiscal crisis. Administrators must therefore be informed about the nature and extent of the legal protections afforded faculty in the relationship between employee (faculty) and employer (college or university).

The purpose of this report is to identify and analyze those major areas of legal protection for faculty employees about which administrators must be aware. It begins with a broad perspective on judicial involvement in academic decisions about faculty employment and continues with in-depth analyses of four broad areas affecting higher education. Those four broad areas—employment practices, equal pay, developing issues under Title IX, and financial exigency—are salient to higher education and, in particular, to the managerial discretion and flexibility needed to cope with the effect of diminishing resources. The monograph thus analyzes the legal protections that administrators must honor, but it also describes areas where managerial discretion and flexibility are relatively unaffected by these laws. The analysis and guidelines are not a list of "don'ts"; they are rather suggestions for positive and legally sound administrative action.

Employment Practices
A key issue of the 1980s is litigation challenging discrimination in employment under Title VII of the Civil Rights Act of 1964, as amended by the Education Amendments of 1972, which prohibits discrimination in employment based on race, color, religion, sex, or national origin. The primary agency for enforcing this legislation is the Equal Employment Opportunity Commission (EEOC). Court cases indicate the courts' deference to academic autonomy in selection and promotion of faculty as long as criteria and selection processes are free of discrimination and meet the intent of the law (Aiken 1976; Hendrickson and Mangum 1977, p. 32).

Equal Pay
Salary decisions facing administrators in austere times involve questions regulated by the Equal Pay Act of 1963, which mandates pay scales that do not differentiate on the basis of sex. Acceptable criteria in differentiating salaries include skills required, level of responsibilities, seniority, incentives, or other factors not related to sex (Aiken 1976, p. 279).

Developing Issues under Title IX
Another issue influencing employment decisions in the 1980s is Title IX of the Education Amendments of 1972. Although it is clear that this statute covers institutional policies on admissions, recruitment of students, institutional publications, textbooks, and athletics (Hendrickson and Mangum 1977, p. 32), the scope of Title IX's coverage of employment is a continuing controversy. The regulations clearly state that employment is implied within the legislation:

No person shall, on the basis of sex, be excluded from participation in, be denied the benefits of, or be subjected to discrimination in employment, or recruitment, consideration, or selection therefor, whether full-time or part-time, under any education program or activity operated by a recipient which receives or benefits from Federal financial assistance [34 C.F.R. §106.51 (a)(1)].

The Supreme Court upheld these regulations in a recent case, *North Haven* v. *Bell* [456 U.S. 512 (1982)], but the scope of coverage or program specificity of Title IX within the institution and what constitutes financial assistance are still pending before the Court in *Grove City* v. *Bell* [687 F.2d 684 (3d Cir. 1982), *cert. granted,* 51 U.S.L.W. 3611 (Feb. 22, 1983)]. The advantage of Title IX to individuals challenging discrimination in employment is that it eliminates the cumbersome administrative requirements of an EEOC investigation and permits direct private action. Courts may be very reluctant to cut off federal funds, however, the remedy under Title IX, therefore suggesting that filing suit under Title IX may be more of a pressure tactic employed by litigants than an effective mechanism for obtaining individual relief from sex discrimination.

Financial Exigency
Facing financial exigencies and retrenchment is a fact of life.

Faculty and administrators must address policy questions on retrenchment before the time to retrench arrives. We must make the tough decisions before the crisis hits. This will protect institutions from costly litigation and provide them with better cases when they have to go to court. It will also help to insure that institutions have fair and equitable methods at hand for making hard choices (Hendrickson 1982, p. 341).

Retrenchment and reductions in faculty must involve questions of retirement and attrition. The Age Discrimination in Employment Act of 1967 states:

It shall be unlawful for an employer (1) to fail or refuse to hire or to discharge any individual or otherwise

*discriminate against any individual with respect to his
compensation, terms, conditions, or privileges of
employment, because of such individual's age; (2) to
limit, segregate, or classify his employees in any way
which would deprive or tend to deprive any individual of
employment opportunities or otherwise adversely affect
his status as an employee because of such individual's
age; or (3) to reduce the wage rate of any employee in
order to comply with this Act [29 U.S.C. §621–34 (1970)].*

This legislation raised the mandatory retirement age to 70
in the 1978 amendments [29 U.S.C. §621–34 (1981)].
Although colleges and universities were exempt from this
legislation through June 30, 1980, the implications for
raising the mandatory retirement age are clear. "If all
faculty members in the country work until age 70—as the
Age Discrimination in Employment Act of 1967 now
entitles them to do—many institutions of higher education
will have few, if any, tenured positions open in the next ten
years" (Guthrie 1982). While federal legislation is pending
that would exempt higher education, another bill would
eliminate the mandatory retirement age altogether (*Chronicle* 1982a). A case brought by Wyoming challenges the
right of the federal government to set the retirement age of
state employees; plaintiffs argued orally before the Supreme Court that the right is reserved by the Constitution
to the states (*Chronicle* 1982c).

Although the legal issues this report addresses are
important ones, other areas of employment law may also
affect decisions about employment in higher education.
This report, for example, does not address the issue of
collective bargaining; an agreement so negotiated may
prescribe or limit the manner in which employment decisions are made on a particular campus. It does not examine the developing law concerning sex-based pensions,
which may shortly have important ramifications for higher
education. Employment law is complex, and administrators are well advised to consult legal counsel before
making significant changes in employment practices.

Judicial Approach To Faculty Employment Decisions

Until the 1970's, litigation involving higher education institutions was infrequent; it was often initiated by the college itself in an attempt to preserve academic freedom and autonomy. The *Dartmouth College* case [*Trustees of Dartmouth College* v. *Woodward,* 4 Wheat. (U.S.) 518 (1819)], in which New Hampshire unsuccessfully sought to alter the college's charter, and the famous victory for academic freedom in *Sweezy* v. *New Hampshire* [354 U.S. 234 (1957)], in which a legislative attempt to question a professor about the content of his class lecture was prohibited, are good examples of the subject matter and disposition of early court cases involving higher education. Judges accorded great deference to the decisions of administrators and faculty, for the courts viewed higher education as a privilege rather than a right, and judges believed themselves unqualified to review or modify decisions concerning academic matters (Kaplin 1978, pp. 4–7).

Social changes during the 1960s, however, brought the courts into more frequent contact with colleges and universities. Postsecondary education became an important path to upward mobility, and new federal policies attempted to make a college degree widely available rather than a privilege reserved only for those who could afford it. In addition to this shift in societal attitudes toward college, the sweeping civil rights legislation passed during the mid-1960s resulted in increased litigation involving colleges. Disaffected students and faculty members now had judicial avenues through which to challenge the decisions of colleges and universities. Escalating fiscal pressures and a stagnant job market for faculty stimulated lawsuits over negative employment decisions. The reaction of higher education administrators to the increased litigation was understandably negative. Litigation was not only costly and time-consuming; it also encouraged confrontation, and many administrators believed that the courts would weaken or destroy collegiality, peer review, and academic freedom.

Several court rulings during the late 1970s and early 1980s might suggest that judicial review has the potential to curtail collegial decision making and peer review. A federal judge in Pennsylvania granted "conditional tenure" to an assistant professor denied tenure at Muhlenberg College [*Kunda* v. *Muhlenberg College, 621 F.2d 532 (3d Cir.*

1980)]. In the newly created Eleventh Circuit, a professor at the University of Georgia was jailed for 90 days and fined $3,000 for refusing to reveal how he voted in a tenure decision [*In re: Dinnan,* 661 F.2d 426 (11th Cir. 1981)]. The Ninth Circuit found that a French department's disparagement of feminist studies as a scholarly discipline was per se sex discrimination [*Lynn* v. *Regents of the University of California,* 656 F.2d 1337 (9th Cir. 1981)]. And a federal district court judge in Montana ordered an overhaul of the governance and peer review system at Montana State University because no women participated in the process [*Mecklenberg* v. *Board of Regents of Montana State University,* 13 Empl. Prac. Dec. ¶11,438 (D. Mont. 1976)].

It is unquestionable that federal and state courts wield considerable power and that litigation has the potential to interfere with the management and policy making of postsecondary institutions. Yet a careful analysis of litigation over faculty employment matters reveals very few instances of "judicial intervention" and numerous examples of judicial deference to academic discretion (Hobbs 1981). Judicial opinions over the last decade indicate that, while they have carefully reviewed employment decisions alleged to be discriminatory, courts have upheld the right of colleges to base employment decisions on subjective judgments of quality and performance and have focused their attention on the fairness of the decision-making procedures.

[C]areful analysis of litigation over faculty employment matters reveals very few instances of "judicial intervention". . . .

The Posture of the Courts in Faculty Employment Litigation
Despite the marked escalation in litigation by faculty challenging negative employment decisions, faculty plaintiffs have prevailed in relatively few cases. This section briefly describes the method of judicial review for several areas of faculty employment litigation, comments upon potential or actual "intervention" by the courts in academic decision making, and examines the degree of deference shown by the courts to the procedures and substantive criteria used to make employment decisions in academe.

Termination of tenured faculty
In reviewing terminations of tenured faculty for cause, courts have generally required only that the procedures

used to terminate the individual be fair (for example, that the hearing be impartial, that the faculty member be permitted to question witnesses) [*Poterma* v. *Ping,* 462 F. Supp. 328 (S.D. Ohio 1978)]. Because tenure gives a faculty member a property right in his or her job, termination may only be for "cause," and the faculty member must be given an opportunity for a hearing [*Perry* v. *Sinderman,* 408 U.S. 593 (1972)]. A "property right" in one's job means that a faculty member is legitimately entitled to remain in that position absent unusual circumstances and furthermore that the faculty member's employment may not be terminated without notice and a hearing. "Cause" is usually defined as incompetence, neglect of duty, or moral turpitude, although the institution's policy statements may include additional definitions of "cause." Generally, courts have not attempted to review the wisdom or accuracy of the decision to terminate a tenured faculty member; rather they defer to the judgment of the college's faculty and administration. In an often-quoted opinion, the Third Circuit stated that "the administration of the internal affairs of a college and especially the determination of professional competency is a matter peculiarly within the discretion of a college administrator" [*Chung* v. *Park,* 514 F.2d 382 (3d Cir. 1975)]. The court added that the purpose of judicial review of the hearing and other procedural protections was not to determine the wisdom of the decision but to ascertain whether it was made fairly. Another federal court reviewing a tenured faculty member's termination cautioned that courts should not review the merits of the termination because such review would intrude upon the college's internal affairs [*Ferguson* v. *Thomas,* 430 F.2d 852 (5th Cir. 1970)]. In sum, where tenured faculty are terminated for cause, judicial review is overwhelmingly deferential as long as the college afforded the faculty member adequate procedural safeguards.

Even in the dismissal of tenured faculty for reasons of financial exigency, the courts have required only that colleges show that their declaration of financial exigency was made in good faith [*AAUP* v. *Bloomfield College,* 346 A.2d 615 (N.J. 1975)]. Courts have refused, however, to second-guess the administration's choice of particular faculty to be terminated, saying that it is "peculiarly within the province of the administration to determine which teachers should be released, and which should be re-tained" [*Levitt* v. *Board of Trustees of Nebraska State Colleges,* 376 F. Supp. 945 (D. Neb. 1974), p. 950]. Even in cases where faculty plaintiffs alleged that the administra-tion's dislike of the faculty member's personal views motivated the termination (potentially a violation of both academic freedom and more general First Amendment rights), courts have held that administrative discretion in the face of financial exigency is broad, and unless a plain-tiff can prove actual bias on the part of administrators, any termination supported by a rational basis and made in good faith will generally be upheld [see, for example, *Bignall* v. *North Idaho College,* 538 F.2d 243 (9th Cir. 1976)].

Termination of untenured faculty

The deference of the judiciary to employment decisions made by academics is especially evident in litigation concerning the termination of untenured faculty. Absent evidence of some violation of constitutional rights by the college, the untenured faculty member need be given neither a hearing nor a statement of reasons for the deci-sion not to rehire [*Board of Regents* v. *Roth,* 408 U.S. 564 (1972)]. Because untenured faculty members had no legitimate expectation for continued employment, the court reasoned, such faculty members did not have the "property right" protection tenured faculty enjoy. Thus, the simple nonrenewal of a contract does not reach consti-tutional significance. Even in cases where untenured faculty had been promised that tenure would be awarded "as a matter of course" by a chairperson or dean [*Davis* v. *Oregon State University,* 591 F.2d 493 (9th Cir. 1978)] or where the decision to deny tenure was based upon misrep-resentations about the plaintiff made by an administrator [*Papadopoulos* v. *Oregon State Board of Higher Educa-tion,* 511 P.2d 854 (Ore. 1973)], courts have generally refused to review the merits of the decision, much less to overturn the decision. In a few cases, courts have over-turned dismissals of nontenured faculty after finding that the college violated the faculty member's right of free speech [see, for example, *Endress* v. *Brookdale Commu-nity College,* 364 A.2d 1080 (N.J. Super., A.D., 1976)] or because the professor had not been permitted to refute the charges of racism that occasioned his dismissal [*Wellner* v.

Minnesota State Junior College Board, 487 F.2d 153 (8th Cir. 1973)]. While courts generally have not permitted colleges to fire untenured faculty who can prove that their dismissal was in retaliation for constitutionally protected speech, courts have upheld the discharge of untenured faculty who made statements that disrupted the management of the college [see, for example, *Duke* v. *North Texas State University,* 469 F.2d 829 (5th Cir. 1972)]. If a college can prove that a nontenured faculty member is uncooperative and troublesome, a court ruled, a faculty member "does not immunize himself against [the] loss of his position simply because his noncooperation and aggressive conduct are verbalized" [*Chitwood* v. *Feaster,* 468 F.2d 359 (4th Cir. 1972), p. 361]. Criticism of administration and faculty in front of students by an untenured faculty member was not constitutionally protected speech, a federal court ruled, for "we do not conceive academic freedom to be a license for uncontrolled expression at variance with established curricular contents and internally destructive of the proper functioning of the institution" [*Clark* v. *Holmes,* 474 F.2d 928 (7th Cir. 1972), p. 931]. While more recent cases have tended to protect the free speech of faculty, the *Chitwood* and *Clark* cases appear still to be good law.

Denials of promotion/tenure/renewal alleging discrimination

The courts continued their pattern of deference to academic decision making in early litigation in which faculty members alleged that a negative employment decision had been motivated by discrimination rather than by evaluation of the individual's qualifications. In nonacademic employment discrimination cases, courts were much more likely to examine the substance of the decision when a plaintiff alleged that the decision was discriminatory. In such a case, the plaintiff must assert that, "but for" the use of an illegal criterion for the decision (such as the plaintiff's race, sex, national origin, religion, or age), the employment decision would have been positive. Alleging that the decision not to promote, grant tenure to, or renew a faculty member was discriminatory requires a court to examine the decision to ascertain what criteria were used to make the decision and whether they were applied fairly in the plaintiff's case.

In early employment discrimination cases in academe, courts were most reluctant to inquire into the merits of the employment decision, believing that the courts were not competent to review employment decisions made by academics [*Faro* v. *New York University,* 502 F.2d 1229 (2d Cir. 1974), pp. 1231–32]. The same court later rejected its earlier hands-off approach, however, and another federal court asserted that "the fact that the discrimination in this case took place in an academic rather than a commercial setting does not permit the court to abdicate its responsibility to insure the award of a meaningful remedy" (*Kunda* v. *Muhlenberg College* 1980, p. 550).

Despite the recent judicial recognition that academic employment decisions should be scrutinized no less closely than employment decisions made in nonacademic organizations, courts generally have left to the academics the decisions as to what evaluative criteria should be used, how they should be weighted, and how they should be applied, focusing their attention instead on the fairness of procedures and whether similarly situated candidates for promotion or tenure were treated equitably. They have only rarely overturned a negative employment decision because the criteria were unclear but have more frequently ruled for plaintiffs where the procedures were biased (*Mecklenberg* v. *Montana State Board of Regents* 1976). In a few cases, courts have overturned denials of promotion or tenure, contending that the decision was a discriminatory one, but generally, if an institution uses fair procedures and can articulate a plausible, nondiscriminatory reason for reaching the decision, the court will find in the college's favor (Lee 1982–83).

Salary disputes

While courts have deferred to academic judgment in decisions concerning hiring, promotion, tenure, or termination, they have been much less deferential to academe in litigation over salaries. The Equal Pay Act of 1963 requires employers to pay female employees the same salary they pay male employees if both sexes perform the same work. Courts have apparently believed themselves more competent to evaluate whether salary decisions have been discriminatory than they have felt themselves to be in reviewing subjective peer review judgments. Litigation alleging salary inequities among male and female faculty members has been complicated and erratic. Sophisticated statistical analysis has been necessary to separate other causes of lower salaries for female faculty (such as fewer years of teaching experience or clustering of women in low-status disciplines) from outright discrimination. While colleges usually prevailed in early cases alleging salary discrimination, federal courts in several recent cases have found salary practices to discriminate against female faculty and have ordered colleges to overhaul their salary structures [see, for example, *Mecklenberg* v. *Montana State Board of Regents* 1976 and *Marshall* v. *Georgia Southwestern College,* 489 F. Supp. 1322 (M.D. Ga. 1980)]. Litigation over salary discrimination has been more successful for faculty plaintiffs than litigation challenging individual decisions about promotion or tenure. Courts are less likely to view the judgments made in salary decisions as presumptively valid, especially where the college has no standard criteria for making individual salary determinations. While litigation over compensation is less likely to threaten peer review and academic autonomy than litigation over promotion and tenure, equal pay litigation may have serious consequences for a college's budget. A college or university sued under the Equal Pay Act has reason for concern, for a finding of discrimination could necessitate paying thousands of dollars in back pay and salary adjustments. The developing law of comparable worth also has implications for colleges in their role as employers (this area of the law is in a very early stage of development and is not discussed in this report).

Areas of Judicial Deference and Scrutiny
An examination of the last decade of litigation over faculty employment disputes makes it clear that, although the potential for judicial intervention in academic decision making is undeniable, the courts have intervened infrequently. Despite their willingness to review peer evaluations in cases where faculty have alleged discrimination by the college, courts have rarely overturned faculty peer determinations. When they have, the courts have found evaluators' misconduct to have been flagrant [see, for example, *Acosta* v. *University of the District of Columbia,* 528 F. Supp. 1215 (D.D.C. 1981) and *Lynn* v. *University of*

California Regents 1981]. In the majority of these cases, however, courts have not found the evidence presented by plaintiffs sufficient to justify legal relief. Courts have upheld the right of faculty to select their own colleagues, to determine the curricular and research missions of their departments, and to evaluate their peers within and without their institutions. In particular, courts have upheld the right of administrators to curtail or eliminate academic programs, lay off tenured faculty, and establish standards for faculty conduct and performance.

It is the decision-making procedures of a college, however, that courts have become more likely to scrutinize. How are candidates for promotion evaluated? Is the decision-making process roughly the same across departments? Are similarly situated persons treated similarly? Are salary decisions made on sex-neutral grounds? Does a college's declaration of fiscal stress evidence good faith?

The ever-declining faculty job market and the escalating fiscal pressures on colleges and universities will encourage more litigation as faculty challenge negative employment decisions. The following four chapters discuss in some detail the four areas of faculty employment where courts have been most active; the final chapter offers guidelines for administrative practice so that litigation may be avoided.

The employment rights of faculty are protected by the plethora of state and federal laws and regulations generally applicable to employees. These laws and regulations protect persons who can show that they were denied some employment benefit to which they were entitled (for example, a promotion or a salary increase) not because they were unqualified but because of arbitrary discrimination based upon their race, gender, religion, national origin, citizenship status, or age. Rather than elaborating upon every law, regulation, and executive order that touches upon faculty civil rights in employment matters, this chapter and the next describe in some detail the federal laws used most frequently by faculty in employment-related litigation against colleges and universities.

Faculty who sue their college or university have quite frequently relied upon three federal laws to challenge a negative employment decision. All three laws forbid discrimination in employment decisions, but the types of people covered by these laws and the remedies the laws provide differ somewhat.

Title VII of the Civil Rights Act of 1964 (42 U.S.C. §2000e *et seq.*) provides the broadest coverage of the three laws and is used with the greatest frequency in litigation by faculty challenging negative employment decisions.

(a) It shall be an unlawful employment practice for an employer—

(1) to fail or refuse to hire or to discharge any individual, or otherwise to discriminate against any individual with respect to his compensation, terms, conditions, or privileges of employment, because of such individual's race, color, religion, sex, or national origin; or

(2) to limit, segregate, or classify his employees or applicants for employment in any way which would deprive or tend to deprive any individual of employment opportunities or otherwise adversely affect his status as an employee, because of such individual's race, color, religion, sex, or national origin (42 U.S.C. §2000e).

Individuals who are successful in a suit under Title VII may recover back pay for a period not to exceed two years prior to the date of filing the complaint with the state agency or the

Equal Employment Opportunity Commission.[1] They may also be reinstated and may, if the court permits, require the defendant employer to pay their attorneys' fees and other costs of litigation.

Section 1981 of the Civil Rights Act, originally passed in 1866, forbids discrimination based upon race or alienage. The law, passed just after the Civil War, states:

> All persons within the jurisdiction of the United States shall have the same right in every State and Territory to make and enforce contracts, to sue, be parties, give evidence, and to the full and equal benefit of all laws and proceedings for the security of persons and property as is enjoyed by white citizens, and shall be subject to like punishment, pains, penalties, taxes, licenses, and exactions of every kind, and to no other (42 U.S.C. §1981).

Although this law provides protection against discrimination in areas other than employment (such as real estate transactions, for example), it has been used with some frequency by faculty who are members of a racial minority or who are not U.S. citizens to challenge negative employment decisions. Unlike Title VII, Section 1981 does not limit a back pay award to two years, but its other remedial provisions are similar to those of Title VII. The coverage of Section 1981 and Title VII overlap, for they both forbid racial discrimination in employment; however, Section 1981 does not cover gender-, religious-, or national origin–based discrimination, while Title VII does not forbid discrimination on the basis of citizenship.

The third law prohibiting employment discrimination in colleges and universities is Title IX of the Education Amendments of 1972 (20 U.S.C. §1681 *et seq.*), which forbids gender-based discrimination in educational institutions. Because the coverage of Title IX is broader than employment and because its remedies differ considerably from those

Title VII . . . is used with the greatest frequency in litigation by faculty challenging negative employment decisions.

In actuality, back pay awards often total more than two years' salary because of protracted litigation. Should the plaintiff prevail and be reinstated, a back pay award could include pay for the two years prior to filing the complaint plus pay for all the time that elapsed before the plaintiff was reinstated (less mitigating amounts earned by the plaintiff from other employment).

---

provided by Title VII and Section 1981, Title IX is discussed separately in a later chapter.

Although Title VII and Section 1981 protect somewhat different groups, their remedies are similar and their litigation requirements, in terms of burdens of proof and the types of evidence needed to prove a case of employment discrimination under each law, nearly identical. Therefore, although this discussion focuses upon Title VII, readers should understand that the discussion also applies, except where indicated, to litigation under Section 1981 as well.[2]

This chapter first describes the order of proof and the burdens of proof for both plaintiffs and defendant colleges in academic Title VII cases. The chapter then describes the general attitude of the federal courts toward employment discrimination litigation involving colleges and universities, especially in regard to their approach to peer evaluations. Next, the chapter describes how courts review decision-making *procedures* and decision-making *criteria* in these academic Title VII cases. The discussion then turns to the type of reasons for negative employment decisions that courts have ruled are permissible and nondiscriminatory. Several cases of "reverse discrimination" are noted briefly, and the chapter ends with an examination of special problems related to using confidential peer evaluations as evidence in academic employment litigation.

Elements of a Title VII Case
It is useful first to summarize the three elements of a Title VII case. The requirements for both plaintiffs and defendants have been well established after a decade of such litigation, and the failure of one of the parties to produce the type of evidence required for each step of the case could result in victory for the opposing party.

In all litigation, whether civil or criminal, the person initiating the litigation has the burden of persuading the

[2]Many states have passed laws forbidding employment discrimination and have also created state agencies to investigate charges of discriminatory employment practices in both the public and private sectors. Where these laws exist, plaintiffs often pursue their state administrative remedies before suing under Title VII. There is no requirement, however, that plaintiffs exhaust their state administrative remedies (other than that they file their initial complaint with the state agency and observe the 60-day deferral period) before pursuing their remedies under Title VII.

fact finder (either a jury or, as in Title VII cases, which do not use a jury, the judge) that he or she has been wronged and deserves to recover against the defendant. This is called the burden of *persuasion,* and it is solely the plaintiff's burden. Both the plaintiff and the defendant, however, have the burden to produce evidence to support their contentions in court. This is called the burden of *production,* and in Title VII cases it shifts from the plaintiff to the defendant and then back to the plaintiff.

Plaintiff's prima facie case

Under Title VII, the plaintiff must present enough evidence to construct what the courts call a prima facie case of discrimination; that is, a plaintiff must produce sufficient evidence to convince the judge that it is plausible to conclude that discrimination motivated the negative employment decision. Should the plaintiff be unable to present sufficient evidence to make a prima facie case of discrimination, the judge may rule for the defendant college without further testimony.

The plaintiff must satisfy a four-part test to complete the prima facie case. For Title VII cases in academe, a plaintiff must show:

a) *That he or she belonged to a class protected by Title VII;*

b) *That the plaintiff sought and was qualified for promotion, tenure, reappointment, etc.;*

c) *That the plaintiff was not promoted, tenured, or reappointed;*

d) *That, in reappointment cases, the college sought applicants of similar qualifications as plaintiff to fill plaintiff's position or, in the case of promotion, the employer had promoted other persons possessing similar qualifications at approximately the same time [Smith v. University of North Carolina, 632 F.2d 316 (4th Cir. 1980), p. 340].*

If the plaintiff has produced enough evidence to demonstrate that the prima facie case requirement is satisfied, then the burden of producing evidence shifts to the defendant college.

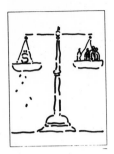

The college's rebuttal

The defendant's burden in a Title VII case requires that the college "articulate some legitimate nondiscriminatory reason" for denying the promotion, tenure, or reappointment to the plaintiff [*Texas Department of Community Affairs* v. *Burdine,* 101 S. Ct. 1089 (1981)]. The U.S. Supreme Court has stated emphatically that it is not necessary for a defendant to prove complete absence of a discriminatory motive in reaching the negative employment decision. Rather, the college needs only to show that a neutral reason, such as inadequacies in the plaintiff's scholarship, teaching, or college service, was a factor in the decision [*Sweeney* v. *Board of Trustees of Keene State College,* 439 U.S. 24 (1978), p. 25]. Generally, if the college can provide evidence that the plaintiff was a poor or marginal teacher or scholar by using evaluations of that teaching or scholarship or by presenting testimony concerning the plaintiff's performance, the college can establish that some factor other than discrimination motivated the negative decision.

The plaintiff's proof of pretext

Once the college has carried its burden, the burden then shifts back to the plaintiff. In this third and final step of a Title VII case, the plaintiff must show that the "legitimate, nondiscriminatory reason" articulated by the defendant college was actually a pretext and that the actual motivation for the decision was a discriminatory one. This final step of the Title VII case is a difficult one for plaintiffs to prove, for they generally must show that the defendant's evidence is false, inadequate, or biased in some way. In the few academic Title VII cases where plaintiffs have prevailed, they have shown that requirements for promotion were applied capriciously [*Kunda* v. *Muhlenberg College,* 621 F.2d 532 (3d Cir. 1980)], that the plaintiff was promoted subsequent to the discriminatory act [*Sweeney* v. *Board of Trustees of Keene State College,* 604 F.2d 106 (1st Cir. 1979], or that the promotion review system that evaluated a plaintiff excluded women and used arbitrary and nonstandard criteria [*Mecklenberg* v. *Board of Regents of Montana State University,* 13 Empl. Prac. Dec. ¶11,438 (D. Mont. 1976)]. These cases are exceptions, however; ordinarily, it is most difficult for a plaintiff to challenge the neutral criteria used in a negative employment decision.

The requirements of an academic Title VII case demonstrate that considerable evaluative evidence concerning the plaintiff's qualifications and job performance must be introduced by both parties in their efforts to justify their positions. The nature of this evidence and some of the problems related to using peer review evaluations in litigation are discussed later in this chapter.

The Courts' Attitude toward Academic Employment Discrimination Cases

While this report focuses primarily on present law and practice rather than on a historical perspective, it is useful for faculty and administrators to understand how the attitude of the federal courts toward academic Title VII cases has shifted over the last decade. The courts approached early academic Title VII litigation with great hesitancy, for the judges believed it inappropriate for the judiciary to intervene in the internal affairs of a college or university. The U.S. Court of Appeals for the Second Circuit made a strong statement to that effect, saying that "of all fields which the federal courts should hesitate to invade and take over, education and faculty appointments at a university level are probably the least suited for federal court supervision" [*Faro* v. *New York University,* 502 F.2d 1229 (2d Cir. 1974), pp. 1231–32]. Another court believed that the judiciary was not competent to examine employment decisions in academe: "Courts are not qualified to review and substitute their judgment for the subjective, discretionary judgments of professional experts on faculty promotions" [*Clark* v. *Whiting,* 607 F.2d 634 (4th Cir. 1979), p. 640]. Other early cases refused to review the professional judgments of college faculty concerning the abilities of their peers [*Green* v. *Board of Regents,* 474 F.2d 594 (5th Cir. 1973), p. 596]. The courts in these early cases believed that judicial review was improper because the court would be required to go beyond its own expertise to evaluate the judgments of faculty. The courts did not address the question of whether review procedures were fair, whether similarly situated faculty were reviewed in a manner similar to the plaintiff's review, or whether independent evidence of discrimination, apart from the review of promotion or tenure, was present.

More recent cases have shown courts to be somewhat less deferential to the decisions made within colleges and universities. Moreover, the courts have discussed the need to view postsecondary institutions as they would any other employer of professionals (Waintroob 1979–80). For example, the U.S. Court of Appeals for the Second Circuit, which had eschewed judicial scrutiny in the *Faro* case cited earlier, repudiated that stance four years later, explaining that the earlier "anti-interventionist policy has rendered colleges and universities virtually immune to charges of employment bias," and promised in the future not to "rely on any such policy of self-abnegation where colleges are concerned" [*Powell* v. *Syracuse University,* 580 F.2d 1150 (2d Cir. 1978), p. 1153]. In a recent opinion, the U.S. Court of Appeals for the Third Circuit made the point more strongly, seemingly exploding the theory that academic employment decisions should be exempt from the same kind of judicial scrutiny afforded employment discrimination claims arising in nonacademic organizations.

> *The fact that the discrimination in this case took place in an academic rather than commercial setting does not permit the court to abdicate its responsibility to insure the award of a meaningful remedy. Congress did not intend that those institutions which employ persons who work primarily with their mental faculties should enjoy a different status under Title VII than those which employ persons who work primarily with their hands (Kunda v. Muhlenberg College 1980, p. 550).*

The courts' willingness to scrutinize academic employment decisions more closely, while requiring defendant colleges to produce more evidence, has not, however, resulted in "judicial intervention" into a college's decision-making process. In this regard, a federal court warned that judges should "steer a careful course between excessive intervention in the affairs of the university and the unwarranted tolerance of unlawful behavior" (*Powell* v. *Syracuse University* 1978, p. 1154). One commentator believes that the concern over judicial deference or the more recent closer judicial scrutiny is inappropriate and that courts have not taken the hands-off approach of which they have been accused.

> *One can question whether the cases . . . in which plaintiffs have not succeeded in proving sex discrimination against a college or university really result from "hands off" approaches to academic personnel decisions or instead reflect a lack of evidence of sex discrimination. While some courts have expressed rhetorical reservations about "second-guessing" the peer review process in higher education, it is clear that in most of the cases . . . the courts conducted thorough reviews of the evidence to ascertain whether sex discrimination occurred* (Flygare 1980–81, p. 105).

Nevertheless, in recent opinions, courts have stated their intention to "look beyond the facade of peer review" and treat academic personnel decisions with the same scrutiny as those made in other kinds of organizations (Flygare 1980–81, p. 106). Despite the increased judicial scrutiny and the determination to treat academic employment no differently from employment in other settings, the courts have continued to protect peer review evaluations. In the *Kunda* case, where the court stressed that colleges were not exempt from judicial scrutiny, the court identified the element of an academic employment decision to which it would continue to defer: "Determinations about such matters as teaching ability, research, scholarship, and professional stature are subjective, and unless they can be shown to have been used as the mechanism to obscure discrimination, they must be left for evaluation by the professionals" (*Kunda* v. *Muhlenberg College* 1980, p. 548). In other words, the court implies that peer review determinations enjoy a presumption of accuracy unless a plaintiff can demonstrate that such determinations were a pretext for discrimination.

Judicial Scrutiny of Decision Procedures

In reviewing decisions challenged by plaintiffs, whether employment-related or not, courts often distinguish between the procedures used to make a decision on the one hand and the actual substance of the decision and the criteria upon which the decision was based on the other hand. Frequently, a court will agree to review decision-making procedures but will declare the substance of a decision and its supporting criteria to be unreviewable because such matters are within the discretion of organizational decision makers.

Judicial reluctance to second-guess the determinations of professionals is not limited to colleges and universities. "As a court's estimation of a particular job's mental difficulty, communication and educational requirements, prestige, and social importance increases, the more apt it becomes to require complex, particularized, and convincing evidence" before it will overturn a negative employment decision (Waintroob 1979–80, pp. 46–47). Furthermore, in reviewing white collar employment decisions alleged to be discriminatory, courts are less likely to overturn subjective evaluations than they are to rule against unfair or biased evaluation procedures (p. 49). Thus, the distinction between decision-making *procedures* and decision-making *criteria* is not unique to litigation involving higher education.

In recent academic employment discrimination litigation, the federal courts have to some degree reviewed the procedures used to reach decisions on promotion, tenure, reappointment, or other employment-related matters. With one exception, to be discussed later, the courts have not found the procedures themselves to be unfair, nor have the courts attempted to dictate the procedures that colleges should use. In the few cases where plaintiffs have challenged the fairness of the procedures themselves, the courts have generally responded that a multilevel review procedure with several decision points and numerous participants is clearly fair [*LaBorde* v. *Regents, University of California,* 495 F. Supp. 1067 (C.D. Cal. 1980); *Smith* v. *University of North Carolina* 1980].

Nor have most courts required colleges to notify plaintiffs of the criteria used to evaluate them or even, in a few cases, that the review was being conducted. For example, a court did not consider it important that, in one case, an individual was evaluated for tenure without being advised of such a review and without being permitted to provide information for the reviewers to consider [*Johnson* v. *University of Pittsburgh,* 435 F. Supp. 1328 (W.D. Pa.

1977)]. When the plaintiff in another case complained to the court that she had never been advised of the criteria for reappointment and that in fact no standards or written criteria were in existence, the court excused the defendant's behavior, saying that the plaintiff should have made herself aware of the university's expectations (*Smith* v. *University of North Carolina* 1980). Another federal court, however, found in the plaintiff's favor and granted her both a promotion and conditional tenure because the college had not advised her that a terminal degree was required for the promotion she sought (*Kunda* v. *Muhlenberg College* 1980).

In addition to a generally permissive scrutiny of decision-making procedures, courts have usually not penalized defendant colleges for failing to warn a plaintiff that his or her performance was inadequate before terminating that individual's employment (see, for example, *Powell* v. *Syracuse University* 1978). Courts have noted with approval, however, instances where college administrators or department heads have warned plaintiffs repeatedly about inadequate scholarship, teaching, or college service [*Lieberman* v. *Gant*, 630 F.2d 60 (2d Cir. 1980); *Peters* v. *Middlebury College*, 409 F. Supp. 857 (D. Vt. 1976)]. There is no question that a defendant college's litigation position is considerably stronger if it can show a record over several years of notifications to the plaintiff that his or her performance was inadequate.

[M]ost courts [have not] required colleges to notify plaintiffs of the criteria used to evaluate them. . . .

One exception to the generally permissive judicial scrutiny of decision-making procedures deserves mention at this point. In *Mecklenberg* v. *Montana State Board of Regents*, the plaintiffs challenged the promotion and tenure review procedures at Montana State University, calling them arbitrary because they were not standardized and discriminatory because women were excluded from the review process. The trial court agreed, saying that the decision procedures and criteria were so imprecise that they permitted decision makers to use "a number of vague and subjective standards . . . [and that] there [were] no safeguards in the procedure to avert sex discriminatory practices" (1976, p. 6495). In its order, the trial court required the university to completely overhaul its governance and peer review process to make it more democratic and more objective. No other court, before or since this case, has required such a substantial revision of review procedures; therefore, *Mecklenberg* may be more of a curiosity than a harbinger of future judicial action.

Some commentators have criticized the opinion in *Mecklenberg* for "its unrestrained invasion of the universally accepted academic selection process at all the faculty and administrative levels of the institution" (Adams and Hall 1976, p. 228). Adams and Hall were especially critical of the judge's refusal to exhibit the standard judicial deference to peer review evaluations exhibited in most academic employment discrimination cases. Whether or not *Mecklenberg* is good or bad law, it has yet to be followed in subsequent academic Title VII cases.

Court Review of Peer Review Criteria
While the courts' review of procedures for promotion and tenure decisions is usually deferential, judicial review of the general criteria used by colleges and universities to evaluate faculty members is even more deferential. Generally speaking, courts are more likely to review the fairness or reasonableness of the application of the decisional criteria than evaluate the relevance or appropriateness of the criteria themselves.

The normal practice of federal courts in employment discrimination cases is to evaluate the criteria used to reach employment decisions to ascertain whether the criteria used act as built-in headwinds and disfavor minority job applicants or employees [*Griggs* v. *Duke Power Co.*, 401 U.S. 424 (1971)]. Although such a review generally is done in class action cases where protected classes allege discriminatory impact rather than the intentional discrimination alleged by most individual faculty plaintiffs, such a review would not be inappropriate in cases where plaintiffs allege that decision makers placed excessive weight on some employment criteria and undervalued the plaintiff's performance on other criteria. For example, plaintiffs have charged that academic decision makers overemphasized the importance of scholarship and research and undervalued the plaintiff's teaching performance and service to the profession or to the institution.

Courts have uniformly refused to examine the importance of the decision-making criteria used by colleges to evaluate faculty.[3] A few have accepted expert testimony as to the relevance and importance of scholarship, research, and service to the functioning of a college or university [*Johnson* v. *University of Pittsburgh* 1977, p. 1356; *Cussler* v. *University of Maryland,* 430 F. Supp. 602 (D. Md. 1977), p. 606]. In other cases, courts have accepted the promotion or tenure criteria listed in the faculty handbook virtually without question, perhaps assuming although not articulating that the handbook was an employment contract between the college and the faculty and that the faculty were on notice of the decisional criteria. The range of judicial review varies from conclusory statements that scholarship, teaching effectiveness, and service are "reasonable and bear a rational relationship to the duties of a college instructor" (*Peters* v. *Middlebury College* 1976, p. 867) to the view by one Federal District Court that, because neither Title VII itself nor the administrative regulations interpreting Title VII provide decisional criteria, a university's established promotion and tenure criteria are "controlling" [*EEOC* v. *Tufts,* 421 F. Supp. 152 (D. Mass. 1975), p. 158].

Such judicial deference to these criteria for promotion and tenure is not surprising, except to those who believe that the courts have become "super tenure review committees" [*Keddie* v. *Pennsylvania State University,* 412 F. Supp. 1264 (M.D. Pa. 1976)]. Plaintiffs have generally not attacked the validity of the criteria themselves but the interpretation and weight given to certain criteria. In the few instances where plaintiffs have challenged the legality of objective criteria (such as possessing a terminal degree), courts have been equally deferential to the judgments of academics. For example, in *Scott* v. *University of Delaware* [20 Empl. Prac. Dec. ¶30,027 (3d Cir. 1979)], a black professor charged that requiring a candidate for tenure to possess a doctoral degree had a disproportionately unfavorable impact on blacks. The court in *Scott* had little difficulty finding that a doctoral degree was related to the mission and needs of the university and upheld the requirement. Similarly, in *Campbell* v. *Ramsey* [22 Fair Empl.

[3]Generally, teaching, scholarship, and service to the college or the profession are the criteria used to evaluate faculty (Centra 1980).

Prac. Cases 83 (E.D. Ark. 1980)], the court found that requiring graduate faculty to hold a doctoral degree was reasonable and was not a pretext for discrimination (p. 84).[4] Furthermore, courts attempted to determine whether a college's criteria for promotion and tenure relate to all the responsibilities of a faculty member, such as advising students, guiding theses and dissertations, or participating in college governance. The courts have recognized that "[a]ll a court can do is to determine whether reasonable good faith was shown and whether fair consideration was given to the matter. . . . If the criteria used and the procedures followed were reasonable and rationally related to the decision reached, this is about as far as the court can go" (*Johnson* v. *University of Pittsburgh* 1977, p. 1357).

Judicial Review of Peer Evaluations

Of special concern to faculty and administrators alike is the potential for the courts to alter the substantive peer judgments about the quality of a faculty member's teaching, scholarship, service, intellectual capacity, or other qualities. Clearly, the courts have the power to reverse a peer decision if a plaintiff establishes that discrimination infected the decision process [*Acosta* v. *University of the District of Columbia,* 528 F. Supp. 1215 (D.D.C. 1981)]. Even in those few cases where plaintiffs have prevailed against colleges in Title VII litigation, however, the original peer evaluation of the plaintiff's qualifications was positive, and the negative recommendation occurred at higher administrative levels (*Kunda* v. *Muhlenberg College* 1980; *Sweeney* v. *Board of Trustees of Keene State College* 1979; *Hill* v. *Nettleton* 1978; *Mecklenburg* v. *Montana State Board of Regents* 1976).

Courts hearing academic Title VII cases have been careful to limit their review to procedural and evidentiary matters, treating the substantive peer review evaluation as conclusive unless proven to be completely without merit.

---

[4]In two cases, however, courts have ruled that instituting a requirement for advanced degrees after a faculty member without such a degree was hired was a pretext for discrimination. In both cases, plaintiffs were female physical education professors who were not advised by their department chairs that an advanced degree was required for continued employment [*Kunda* v. *Muhlenberg College* 1980; *Hill* v. *Nettleton,* 455 F. Supp. 514 (D. Col. 1978)].

The courts have recognized that "the weight to be given scholarly writings and their publication in a tenure decision involves judgmental evaluation by those who live in the academic world . . . and who are charged with the responsibility of the decision" [*Labat* v. *Board of Higher Education,* 401 F. Supp. 753 (S.D.N.Y. 1975), p. 757]. The courts' disinclination to determine the wisdom or accuracy of the substantive peer evaluation is nearly unanimous. In *Sweeney* v. *Board of Trustees of Keene State College,* the court declared that "the recommendation of the [peer review committee] is entitled to stand even if it appears to have been misguided, unless it was sex biased (1979, p. 112). Another court explained its approach even more baldly: "As far as the federal court is concerned, the state could deny tenure to the plaintiff for no reason, a reason based on erroneous facts, or for any reason it chose, except for a reason that violated the plaintiff's constitutional rights" [*Megill* v. *Board of Regents,* 541 F.2d 1073 (5th Cir. 1976), p. 1077].[5]

In two recent academic Title VII cases, the courts found peer evaluations to be biased and therefore found the denial of tenure or promotion to have been motivated by discrimination. Careful reading of the cases, however, reveals that the court was reviewing the fairness with which the criteria were applied rather than the accuracy of the substantive judgment. In *Acosta* v. *University of the District of Columbia* (1981), the court found that the promotion review committee applied evaluation standards arbitrarily in its review of the teaching experience and publications of a Hispanic professor when compared with that committee's evaluation of black faculty members and did not follow established procedures in evaluating the plaintiff. The court ruled that the numerous inconsistencies between the evaluation of the plaintiff and the evaluations of other candidates for promotion or tenure indicated that the plaintiff had been discriminated against (1981, pp. 1220, 1223).

In *Lynn* v. *Regents of the University of California* [656 F.2d 1337 (9th Cir. 1981)], a federal court also found a peer

[5]Although the *Megill* case was litigated under §1983 of the Civil Rights Act, the reasoning used by the court applies with equal force to Title VII litigation.

evaluation to be discriminatory. The plaintiff's scholarship was in the area of women's studies; the court had found that the peer review committee reached its negative decision primarily as a result of its belief that women's studies was not a legitimate field of scholarship. The court concluded that disdain for women's studies as a scholarly pursuit "and a diminished opinion of those who concentrate on those issues, is evidence of a discriminatory attitude toward women" (p. 1343). The court did not rule that such evidence would be sufficient to prove the decision to be a discriminatory one; it merely suggested that disdain for women's studies was an impermissible criterion upon which to base an employment decision. The case is still being litigated, and no final determination has been made concerning the legality of the overall evaluation by the plaintiff's peers.

Despite the findings of the courts in *Acosta* and *Lynn,* courts remain deferential to peer evaluations. If a college can demonstrate that it evaluated a plaintiff in the same way that similarly situated faculty were evaluated, that the evaluation was careful and thorough, and that no preconceived prejudices against the field of inquiry chosen by the plaintiff played a role in the decision, it is most likely that the outcome of that peer evaluation will be unchanged by the courts. In other words, if colleges use fair procedures and apply evaluative criteria evenhandedly, it would be extremely difficult for a plaintiff initiating a meritless lawsuit to prevail. On the other hand, if a plaintiff can provide sufficient evidence of a college's bad faith, the plaintiff can prevail. Thus, despite the "special" nature of academic employment decisions and the deference to peer review that some courts have verbalized, Title VII appears to have succeeded, to some degree at least, in providing remedies for unlawful employment decisions without weakening academic autonomy.

Other Factors Involved in Title VII Cases
A few academic employment cases litigated under Title VII have addressed the issue of whether peers may consider the fit between a candidate for promotion or tenure and the candidate's colleagues. In some cases, the mismatch between a candidate's research or teaching interests and the department's mission or focus has been used to justify

denial of promotion or tenure; in others, personality conflicts with peers have been considered in reaching a negative decision. In both instances, courts have upheld the right of faculty to refuse tenure to individuals whose interests or temperament did not fit those of his or her colleagues, as long as such a decision was legitimate and not a pretext for discrimination.

Although it does not appear that courts have permitted defendants to refuse to renew the contracts of professors solely because they could not get along with their colleagues,[6] courts have frequently mentioned the plaintiff's incompatibility with his or her colleagues. An Illinois District Court noted in *Perham* v. *Ladd* that "professional disagreements with members of an academic department are sufficient, nondiscriminatory reasons to deny tenure" [436 F. Supp. 1101 (N.D. Ill. E.D., 1977), p. 1107]. The Second Circuit echoed these sentiments in *Lieberman* v. *Gant*, explaining that "a clash of personalities is not a sufficient basis for liability [under Title VII]; there must be evidence of sex discrimination" [474 F. Supp. 848 (D. Conn. 1979), p. 868; *aff'd,* 630 F.2d 60 (2d Cir. 1980)]. Plaintiffs who were seen by their colleagues as disruptive, abrasive, or abusive toward other faculty received little sympathy and no relief from the courts [see, for example, *LaBorde* v. *Regents, University of California* 1980, where the plaintiff was a "disruptive influence" in the department, and *Jawa* v. *Fayetteville State University,* 426 F. Supp. 218 (E.D. N.C. 1976), in which the plaintiff was "belligerent" and annoyed departmental colleagues]. Nor did the courts award relief to female plaintiffs who called their colleagues "chauvinist pigs" (*Johnson* v. *University of Pittsburgh* 1977) or were "too assertive in manner" about feminist issues (*Peters* v. *Middlebury College* 1976, p. 860). Although defendant colleges in each of these cases alleged that the faculty member's teaching or scholarship was deficient and that promotion or tenure had therefore

[6]The one exception to this statement may be *Van de Vate* v. *Bolling* [379 F. Supp. 925 (E.D. Tenn. N.D., 1974)]. It appears that the department chair failed to rehire a laid-off temporary instructor solely because of a "personality clash" between himself and the plaintiff. The court noted that a college's decision not to hire someone who "could not harmoniously perform his or her duties" was well within the college's discretion and did not violate Title VII (p. 929).

been denied, the courts in each of these cases allowed testimony concerning such personal clashes and gave them credence as part of the defendant college's rebuttal.

Courts have also found a candidate's compatibility with the academic needs of his or her department to be an evaluative criterion sufficient to rebut a prima facie case of discrimination. Such a criterion has been applied in two ways: In some cases a plaintiff did not have the specialized knowledge or training necessary to meet enrollment demands or shifts in departmental emphasis; in other cases the plaintiff's specialized research did not fit the department's self-identified mission.

Courts have readily accepted the statements of defendant colleges that a plaintiff's specialization did not meet the staffing needs of the department. In *Peters* v. *Middlebury College*, the college argued that the plaintiff could not adequately teach the upper-level English courses for which she had been hired (1976, p. 860). The plaintiff in *Perham* v. *Ladd* had been hired to teach secondary school math but focused her research efforts in elementary math (1977, p. 1107). In *Campbell* v. *Ramsey*, the department's decision to develop a stronger graduate program meant that the plaintiff's lack of a doctorate precluded her from advising and teaching advanced graduate students (1980). And the plaintiff's refusal in *Davis* v. *Weidner* [596 F.2d 726 (7th Cir. 1979), p. 731] to teach income-producing special courses reduced her value to the department to such an extent that it constituted a legitimate nondiscriminatory reason for her termination.

A lack of intellectual compatibility with departmental colleagues also has given courts little pause in finding for defendant colleges. The court in *Johnson* v. *University of Pittsburgh* (1977) agreed that a medical school could terminate a plaintiff with admittedly good research skills because her research interests did not match the mission of the medical school. In *Smith* v. *University of North Carolina*, the Fourth Circuit ruled that the university's statements concerning the plaintiff's intellectual incompatibility with her departmental colleagues were sufficiently nondiscriminatory. The university had argued that the plaintiff did not understand "the meaning of the University and the type of discourse appropriate to it" and that the plaintiff "[did] not [fill] the place within the department which was envisioned at the time of her employment" (1980, p. 326). The court ruled that the department was justified in letting a professor go because it was small and did not have the funds available to support a faculty member who did not contribute to its "growth and development plan," despite the university's admission that the quality of the plaintiff's research itself was adequate (p. 343). Despite the lack of support in academic policy statements (documents of the American Association of University Professors, for example) for denying reappointment, promotion, or tenure on the grounds of personal or professional incompatibility, courts have validated the informal function of peer evaluation as a test of a candidate's ability to conform to the norms and expectations of his or her colleagues (Bergman 1980).

Reverse Discrimination

Early executive orders and certain civil rights laws mandated not only that employers refrain from discriminating against employees but also that they take "affirmative action" to hire a greater proportion of members of underrepresented groups. While the issue of affirmative action in college admissions gained national attention in *Board of Regents* v. *Bakke* 438 U.S. 265 (1978)], the nature and limits of affirmative action in academic employment decisions have also been litigated. Such cases often arise in situations where members of unprotected classes (generally whites and/or males) assert that an employer has hired or promoted a less well-qualified member of a protected class, otherwise known as "reverse discrimination."

The standard of review applied when white and/or majority faculty sue under Title VII alleging reverse race or sex discrimination is identical to that applied when members of minority groups are the plaintiffs. These cases are important primarily because they help to define the outer limits of affirmative action or benign race-conscious employment practices, and brief mention of the courts' approach to such cases is useful. The issues involved where white faculty are employed at predominantly black colleges differ somewhat, however, from the issues sur-

[Reverse discrimination] cases are important primarily because they help to define the outer limits of affirmative action. . . .

rounding race-conscious hiring under an affirmative action plan.

In *Craig* v. *Alabama State University* [451 F. Supp. 1207 (M.D. Ala. 1978)], white faculty alleged that they were discriminated against in hiring and promotion decisions made at the historically black college. Fortunately for the plaintiffs in this case, the administrators charged with employment discrimination had stated candidly a preference for black faculty; statistical evidence also showed a clear pattern of preferential hiring and promotion of blacks. The court reasoned that, although the white plaintiffs had received positive evaluations and were well qualified for their positions, the college president made his own determinations on promotion and hiring, based primarily on racial criteria (p. 1213).

In a second case where a court found reverse discrimination, the contract of a white professor was terminated by the president of Savannah State College, a traditionally black college. The trial court ruled and the appellate court agreed that racial animus and not "academic deficiencies" motivated the termination, and the plaintiff was reinstated with back pay [*Lincoln* v. *Board of Regents of the University System of Georgia*, 697 F.2d 928 (11th Cir. 1983)]. Similar conclusions were reached concerning alleged bias against whites by traditionally black colleges in *Whiting* v. *Jackson State* [616 F.2d 116 (5th Cir. 1980)] and *Fisher* v. *Dillard* [26 Fair Empl. Prac. Cases 184 (E.D. La. 1980)].

Other reverse discrimination cases have alleged that efforts by predominantly white institutions to increase the number of women or minority faculty result in discrimination against whites and/or males. The Community College of Philadelphia had developed an affirmative action plan and sought to increase its proportion of minority faculty. When the college hired two black faculty for full-time positions in art and music, two white women who had been teaching part-time in those two departments and who had applied for the full-time positions, sued under Title VII, claiming reverse discrimination. After a lengthy examination of the credentials of the candidates for both positions, the court concluded that it was reasonable for the college to determine that the minority candidates were better qualified than the plaintiffs and that the plaintiffs' claims were unfounded [*Cohen* v. *Community College of Philadelphia,* 484 F. Supp. 411 (E.D. Pa. 1980)].

Conversely, reverse sex discrimination was found to be present in *Cramer* v. *Virginia Commonwealth University* [415 F. Supp. 673 (D. Va. 1976)]. In seeking candidates for two faculty positions, a department had decided to limit its search to female applicants in an attempt to provide affirmative action. A white male faculty member of lower rank in that department was not permitted to compete for either position, although he was apparently as well qualified as the female candidates. The court held that the college could not condition employment upon gender, despite the national policy supporting affirmative action. The Supreme Court's ruling in *Board of Regents* v. *Bakke* (1978) also suggests that explicit racial or gender-based favoritism, to the exclusion of other races or genders, is not permitted under the Constitution or any law.

Special Problems in Title VII Cases

Although the standard of review used by the courts has become relatively uniform and deference to peer review is the norm, a few issues raised in Title VII litigation have not been resolved and can be quite troublesome for college administrators and faculty. These issues are related to privacy and concern the degree to which a college is inclined to or should preserve the confidentiality of peer evaluations.

To carry its burden of production in establishing that the negative decision was based upon a "legitimate nondiscriminatory reason," colleges often introduce written or oral evaluations of a plaintiff's scholarship, research, or teaching. Occasionally, a reviewer from another institution is required to justify his or her evaluation of the plaintiff; more often, the plaintiff's departmental colleagues must testify concerning the motivations for the determination they made about the plaintiff's qualifications. Sometimes faculty members are asked to evaluate their departmental colleagues or other faculty who are not parties to the case and were not involved in the decision in any way [see, for example, *Ollman* v. *Toll,* 518 F. Supp. 1196 (D. Md. 1981)]. Such an experience may act as a disincentive to further participation in peer evaluations *(California Law Review* 1981).

In other cases, plaintiffs have sought to obtain confidential materials from the peer evaluation because they believe such materials contain evidence of bias. Under federal court rules, such material is clearly relevant to the issue being litigated, and some judges have ordered defendant colleges to give plaintiffs access to all evaluative material upon which the negative decision was based [*Lynn* v. *University of California Regents* 1981; *EEOC* v. *University of New Mexico,* 504 F.2d 1296 (10th Cir. 1974); *Gray* v. *Board of Higher Education,* 692 F.2d 901 (2d Cir. 1982)]. Other courts, however, have refused to require defendant colleges to produce "confidential" material [*McKillop* v. *Regents, University of California,* 386 F. Supp. 1270 (N.D Cal. 1975); *Keyes* v. *Lenoir Rhyne College,* 552 F.2d 579 (4th Cir. 1977), *cert. denied,* 434 U.S. 904 (1977)].

In still other cases, plaintiffs have sought to introduce the peer evaluations of other faculty who were candidates for and granted promotion or tenure at the time that the plaintiff was rejected, as a way of attempting to prove that similarly qualified individuals were treated more favorably than was the plaintiff. In some instances, despite the fact that these comparison faculty were not parties to the case or involved in the decision against the plaintiff in any way, courts have permitted comparisons to be made between successful candidates for promotion or tenure and the plaintiff *(Johnson* v. *University of Pittsburgh* 1977; *Smith* v. *University of North Carolina* 1980; *Kunda* v. *Muhlenberg College* 1980). In other cases, however, courts have refused to compare other faculty with the plaintiff because the judge believed that ascertaining the similarities between faculty members' qualifications was not within the court's expertise *(Clark* v. *Whiting* 1979; *Lieberman* v. *Gant* 1980). Despite the arguments for preserving the confidentiality of personnel records pertaining to nonparty faculty, some courts believe that only through such comparisons can a plaintiff demonstrate that he or she received differential, and thus biased, treatment (North Carolina Law Review 1982, p. 445).

In most civil litigation, any relevant information that a party needs for evidence in a case is usually admissible unless it is protected by an evidentiary privilege. Generall speaking, communications between doctors and their patients, lawyers and their clients, and priests and penitents are protected from disclosure; in some cases, sensitive government documents are protected by an "official information privilege." The rationale for protecting certain information from disclosure is that the public interest is stronger in encouraging open discussion between certain individuals (for example, doctors and patients) or by preserving sensitive government information than the private interest of the individual litigant in obtaining access to the information for which the privilege is sought (Louisell and Mueller 1978).

Courts in recent academic employment discrimination cases have struggled with the question of whether "confidential" peer review evaluations should be protected from disclosure by an "academic freedom privilege" absent strong evidence of discriminatory motive. Unfortunately, federal appeals courts in two circuits have reached opposing conclusions, and the Supreme Court has recently refused to rule on the issue.

When Maija Blaubergs sued the University of Georgia, alleging that sex discrimination motivated a peer review committee's recommendation against tenure, Blaubergs sought to discover the vote of each peer review committee member. Although the university advised him otherwise, Professor James Dinnan refused to reveal how he voted and was found in contempt of court, fined, and jailed for his refusal. Dinnan appealed the contempt charge, citing an "academic freedom privilege" that protected his silence. The U.S. Court of Appeals for the Eleventh Circuit disagreed, saying that such a privilege "would mean that the concept of academic freedom would give any institution *carte blanche* to practice discrimination of all types" *In re: Dinnan,* 661 F.2d 426 (11th Cir. 1981), *cert. denied,* 02 S. Ct. 2904 (1982), p. 431]. The court categorically refused to consider creating an academic freedom privilege, believing the privilege not only unnecessary but harmful:

> *We fail to see how, if a tenure committee is acting in good faith, our decision today will adversely affect its decision-making process. Indeed, this opinion should work to reinforce responsible decision-making in tenure*

*questions as it sends out a clear signal to would-be
wrong-doers that they might not hide behind "academic
freedom" to avoid responsibility for their actions. . . .
[S]ociety has no strong interest in encouraging timid
faculty members to serve on tenure committees* (p. 432).

The U.S. Supreme Court denied review of Dinnan's
appeal; thus, at least in the Eleventh Circuit (Florida,
Georgia, and Alabama), there is no academic freedom
privilege as of this writing.

The U.S. Court of Appeals for the Second Circuit,
however, sees the matter somewhat differently. That court
has approved in principle the use of a qualified academic
freedom privilege but refused to apply it in *Gray* v. *Board
of Higher Education* (1982). In that case, a black male
faculty member had been denied tenure at LaGuardia
Community College (CUNY) and sought to discover the
votes of two tenure committee members. Although the trial
court had approved of and applied the academic freedom
privilege in this case, the appellate court reversed that
determination because the plaintiff had not been given a
statement of reasons for the negative decision. Despite the
fact that the appellate court ruled in the plaintiff's favor, it
approved the concept of an academic freedom privilege
and implied that, had the plaintiff been given a statement of
reasons for the denial of tenure, the court would have
applied the privilege and protected disclosure of the
individual votes. The "privilege" is a qualified one,
requiring the court to balance the plaintiff's need for the
confidential material against the defendant's interest in
preserving its confidentiality. The court, relying upon an
amicus brief prepared by the American Association of
University Professors, endorsed the view that " 'if an
unsuccessful candidate for reappointment or tenure
receives a meaningful written statement of reasons from
the peer review committee and is afforded proper intramu-
ral grievance procedures,' disclosure of individual votes
should be protected by a qualified privilege" (p. 907, citing
AAUP Brief at p. 23). The court continued, declaring that
the privilege "strikes an appropriate balance between
academic freedom and educational excellence on the one
hand and individual rights to fair consideration on the
other" (p. 907). The court's decision "holds that, absent a

statement of reasons, the balance tips toward discovery
[e.g., disclosure] and away from recognition of privilege"
(p. 908). The court made it clear that it would not hesitate
to apply the privilege to protect confidential matters if a
defendant college had followed the proper procedures for
notification.

The Seventh Circuit, in a case that was decided after
both *Dinnan* and *Gray,* refused to apply an academic
freedom privilege to confidential evaluations of a faculty
candidate for tenure. Here, the EEOC was seeking disclosure of the personnel files of other faculty in the candidate's department to ascertain whether the professor's
claim of race discrimination was valid. The Seventh Circuit
did not reject outright the concept of an academic freedom
privilege, as had the Eleventh Circuit. Instead, after
balancing the need of the EEOC for information to aid its
investigation against the university's interest in maintaining
the confidentiality of personnel records, the Seventh
Circuit ruled that in this case no academic freedom privilege protected the information from disclosure [*EEOC* v.
University of Notre Dame du Lac, 551 F. Supp. 737 (7th
Cir. 1982)]. Thus, the Seventh Circuit's view of the existence and propriety of an academic freedom privilege seems
to be closer to the view of the Second Circuit in *Gray* than
the Eleventh Circuit in *Dinnan.* As the Seventh Circuit
decided not to apply the privilege in *Notre Dame,* however, it is not yet clear whether precedent for such a
privilege exists outside the Second Circuit (New York,
Vermont, and Connecticut) or precisely how broad the
coverage of such a privilege might be. Until more federal
appellate courts rule on this issue or the Supreme Court
accepts a case in which this issue is addressed, administrators should tread carefully in the area of the academic
freedom privilege.

Summary

Judicial review of academic employment decisions challenged under Title VII or Section 1981 is evolving toward
greater predictability. Courts are more inclined now than in
the past to examine the fairness and consistency of the
procedures used to make employment decisions and will
examine decision making for evidence of bad faith, arbitrariness, or caprice. Judicial review generally goes no

farther unless overwhelming evidence of deliberate discrimination is present.

Courts generally regard the substantive evaluations of faculty qualifications, especially when conducted by the faculty member's peers, as presumptively valid, again absent overwhelming evidence of misconduct. When the possibility of an academic freedom privilege is added to the substantial deference shown by the courts to academic judgments, it appears likely that an employment decision made in compliance with institutional policies, due process (if applicable), and disciplinary norms would be nearly impervious to challenge unless substantial evidence of bias were available to the plaintiff.

EQUAL PAY: Salary Disputes in Academe

The idea that individuals performing the same job in an organization should receive equal compensation, assuming that they possess equal skill and responsibility, is neither new nor revolutionary. And, unquestionably, equal pay for equal work is the law in this country. The policy is clear and seemingly uncomplicated. Yet the concept of equal pay for college faculty has spawned some of the most complex litigation encountered by the federal courts during the past decade.

The deceptive simplicity of "equal pay for equal work" breaks down when one considers the nature of colleges and universities and the wide variation among individual talents, disciplinary prestige, and scholarly productivity. In addition, like decisions on promotion, tenure, or nonrenewal, evaluations of faculty to determine a starting salary or salary increases are often based upon subjective evaluations of performance or upon abstract notions of what a person trained in a certain discipline is "worth" in the marketplace. Unlike decisions about promotion or tenure, however, where administrators and faculty at many colleges have recognized the need for consistent and carefully documented procedures, the procedures used to make salary determinations are frequently unwritten, ad hoc, and inconsistent from one department to another and from one year to the next.

Such a lack of procedural uniformity and inattention to differential treatment of faculty institutionwide has resulted in colleges' being found liable for substantial back pay and salary adjustment awards to female plaintiffs. In *Mecklenberg* v. *Board of Regents of Montana State University* [13 Empl. Prac. Dec. ¶11,438 (D. Mont. 1976)], the female faculty were eventually awarded nearly $400,000 in salary adjustments (Clark 1977). The University of Minnesota, which entered a consent decree in 1980 in which it agreed to rectify past claims of sex discrimination brought on behalf of all women faculty [*Rajender* v. *University of Minnesota,* 20 Empl. Prac. Dec. ¶30,225 (D. Minn. 1979)], may eventually be required to pay $60 million in salary adjustments and back pay (Wehrwein 1981). Recently, a federal district court found that the City University of New York had discriminated against women professionals (faculty and nonfaculty); although no remedy has been

Unlike decisions about promotion and tenure, . . . procedures used to make salary determinations are unwritten, ad hoc, and inconsistent. . . .

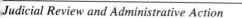

announced at this writing, it could exceed $60 million (McFadden 1983).

The size of the monetary awards and the complexity of the issues involved in litigation are equaled only by the sophistication of the evidentiary issues. Recent cases have relied heavily on regression analysis to prove or disprove the plaintiffs' claims that, when all relevant differentiating factors are statistically controlled, salary differences still existing between male and female faculty can only be a result of sex discrimination. The success of regression analysis for plaintiffs has been mixed, but federal courts are becoming increasingly willing to evaluate complex statistical evidence and to rule against a defendant college if the regression analysis presents sufficiently compelling evidence of salary discrepancies by gender.

This chapter first reviews the statutes used by college faculty to challenge alleged salary discrimination and summarizes the kind of proof each party must provide. It then analyzes relevant cases brought against colleges and universities under these statutes, focusing in particular upon the use of regression analysis in recent equal pay cases in academe. Finally, it discusses some of the problems involved in creating or modifying salary policies and suggests overall trends in judicial review of salary policies in colleges and universities.

Statutory Bases for Salary Discrimination Suits

Two federal statutes provide redress for individuals who allege that their employer discriminates against them by paying them less for equal or comparable work than it pays members of the opposite sex or members of other races, religions, or ethnic groups: Title VII of the Civil Rights Act (42 U.S.C. §2000e *et seq.*) and the Equal Pay Act of 1963 (29 U.S.C.§206). Although colleges and universities were exempted from each of these laws when they were first passed, Congress amended both Title VII and the Equal Pay Act in the Education Amendments of 1972 to apply both civil rights laws to higher education (P. L. 92–318).

Title VII

As indicated in the previous chapter, Title VII prohibits discrimination "against any individual with respect to his compensation, terms, conditions, or privileges of employment" [42 U.S.C. §2000e (1)]. Title VII's protections are broader than those of the Equal Pay Act, for Title VII protects members of racial and ethnic, religious, and national origin minorities. The plaintiff alleging salary discrimination under Title VII need not prove that he or she performs identically equal work, as is required by the Equal Pay Act. Under Title VII, a plaintiff may succeed if he or she can demonstrate that the job used for comparison is comparable, and the Supreme Court has even suggested that persons performing jobs of comparable economic worth to the employer may be entitled to equal pay [see, for example, *County of Washington* v. *Gunther,* 452 U.S. 161 (1981)]. Under Title VII, however, a plaintiff must establish a prima facie case that provides evidence that discrimination is a plausible explanation for the differential salary. Under Title VII, if an employer can prove that the salary differential is a result of business necessity (for example, that local market factors require a business to pay higher salaries to jobs predominantly held by men to guarantee a sufficient supply of employees), then the salary discrepancy may be permitted by the court [*Christensen* v. *State of Iowa,* 563 F.2d 353 (8th Cir. 1977)]. In other words, if a defendant employer can convince the court that the market value of a plaintiff's services rather than a race- or gender-linked characteristic of the plaintiff was responsible for the salary differential, the employer will generally prevail. The court in *Christensen* declared that "nothing in the text and history of Title VII suggest[s] that Congress intended to abrogate the laws of supply and demand or other economic principles that determine wage rates for various kinds of work" (p. 356). Therefore, although the jobs need only be comparable rather than equal under Title VII, plaintiffs suing under Title VII must prove the differential in salary to be squarely attributable to discrimination and not to market factors.

Equal Pay Act

While the Equal Pay Act also provides a remedy for salary discrimination, its approach differs somewhat from that of Title VII. The relevant section of the Equal Pay Act provides that

No employer . . . shall discriminate . . . between employees on the basis of sex by paying wages to employees . . .

at a rate less than the rate at which he pays wages to
employees of the opposite sex . . . for equal work on jobs
the performance of which requires equal skill, effort,
and responsibility, and which are performed under
similar working conditions . . . [29 U.S.C. §206(d)(1)].

The law requires that the jobs being compared under an allegation of salary discrimination be equal in each of four ways: equal skill, equal effort, equal responsibility, and equal working conditions. The jobs must require equal skill, defined in the regulations interpreting the law by such factors as experience, training, education, and ability [29 C.F.R. §800.125 (1980)]. Only those skills necessary to performing the requirements of the job may be considered; for example, unrelated academic degrees or irrelevant work experience could not be considered in making salary determinations (Green 1980–81, p. 208). Equal effort means "the physical or mental exertion needed for the performance of a job" [29 C.F.R. §800.127 (1980)]; that is, the jobs must *require* equal effort rather than employees' actually devoting identical amounts of physical or mental effort to the job. Equal responsibility means that the jobs must be equal in the "degree of accountability required in the performance of the job obligation" [29 C.F.R. §800.129 (1980)]; for example, differences in supervisory duties or regularly required extra duties could justify salary differentials between two otherwise equal jobs (Green 1980–81, p. 210). The requirement that working conditions be similar is relatively unimportant to pay disputes of college faculty, for it refers to inside work versus outside work or unpleasant or onerous work compared with more favorable working conditions.

Once a plaintiff[7] has established the prima facie case that the two positions being compared require equal skill, effort, responsibility, and working conditions, the burden of production shifts to the employer to demonstrate that one of four exceptions listed in the law justifies the salary differential. "When such payment is made pursuant to (i) a seniority system; (ii) a merit system; (iii) a system which

---

[7]Under the Equal Pay Act, the Secretary of Labor investigates claims of salary discrimination and, if evidence of potential discrimination is found, sues on behalf of the affected individuals.

measures earnings by quantity or quality of production; or (iv) a differential based on any factor other than sex" [29 U.S.C. §206(d)(1)], the employer will not be in violation of the Equal Pay Act. Even if the skill, effort, responsibility, and working conditions are identical, salary distinctions may be made between men and women on the basis of the four exceptions included in the law. There has been relatively little dispute in salary cases in academe concerning the legitimacy of seniority or a neutral merit system using objective evaluation criteria. Even an informal merit pay system "will suffice if it can be demonstrated that the standards or criteria applied under it are applied pursuant to an established plan whose essential terms and conditions have been communicated to the affected employees" (Green 1980–81, p. 213). Salary differences based upon the quality or quantity of production have been limited to employees paid commissions or paid at piecework rates and have not been applied to higher education (p. 214). The exception most frequently relied upon by the courts in academic Equal Pay Act cases has been the "factor other than sex" exception. The use of market factors in calculating faculty salaries is an example of this last exemption, and defendant colleges have used it frequently to justify paying women faculty lower salaries than those paid to men. Market differences in the value of a faculty member's services must be supported by strong evidence, however. The college or university must "demonstrate that it actively sought available candidates, that it studied the going market rate, and that it would pay the same dollar amount to a qualified man or woman" (Green 1980–81, p. 215). Estimates or assumptions as to the relative value of a doctorate in English versus a doctorate in computer sciences would not sustain a college's salary disparities under the fourth exception to the Equal Pay Act.

Unlike a salary dispute litigated under Title VII, a plaintiff suing under the Equal Pay Act need not prove discrimination by the employer. If the plaintiff can satisfy the elements of the prima facie case listed earlier and the defendant employer cannot justify the salary discrepancy under one of the act's four exceptions, the plaintiff need go no farther. Because academic salary discrimination cases have been brought under Title VII, the Equal Pay Act, or both, the following discussion focuses primarily on the nature of judicial review of these cases rather than a technical analysis of the evidentiary proof required of each party. Before discussing salary discrimination cases, however, a brief overview of some of the general problems endemic to academic salary decisions will provide background.

Problems in Tracing Causality in Salary Discrimination
Courts, researchers, and litigants alike have struggled with the problems of identifying and separating the factors that present legitimate reasons for salary differentials between men and women from those reasons that are clearly discriminatory. Differences in the behavior of women in the labor market often are used to justify salary or other employment decisions that result in inequity to a particular woman faculty member. In addition, it is often difficult to separate and identify factors that are a result of historical discrimination (for example, a depressed salary history for a middle-aged woman upon which a current salary decision is made) from reasonable, market-related factors used to set a starting salary.

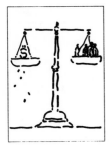

To justify differential salaries, researchers have cited data demonstrating that women devote more time to child care and family responsibilities than do men and that married professional women are less geographically mobile than men because of the potential disruption to a husband's career (Lester 1980, p. 114; Marwell, Rosenfeld, and Spilerman 1979). In addition, the disciplines in which women predominate often tend to have lower status and thus command lower salaries than academic disciplines in which men predominate. According to Koch (1982), 90 percent of all professors of economics in 1975–76 were male, while 50 percent of all English professors in the same year were male, and the market for such faculty differed substantially (p. 8).

Even if women obtain terminal degrees in male-dominated fields, salary or other employment discrimination may continue. Factors such as discriminatory student aid policies, the paucity of female role models or mentors (or the refusal of male faculty to serve as mentors for female graduate students), and the domination of publication or grant networks by males may disfavor female faculty (LaNoue 1982, pp. 8–9). On the other hand, real differences in publication productivity often exist between male and female faculty, especially because women are more likely to be found at colleges that emphasize teaching rather than research (Johnson and Stafford 1974).

Furthermore, it is important that colleges be permitted some flexibility in determining salaries based upon subjective criteria so that a college can attract "star" faculty and prevent its top scholars from leaving by matching the salary offers made by other colleges (LaNoue 1982, p. 12). In cases where colleges can document the exceptional characteristics of highly paid faculty, the "factor other than sex" exception to the Equal Pay Act will apply [see, for example, *Keyes* v. *Lenoir Rhyne College,* 15 Fair Empl. Prac. Cases 914 (W.D.N.C., 1976)]. But where a college cannot document objective factors responsible for salary differences between male and female faculty, and especially where most or all of the individuals making salary decisions are male, a court may conclude that the differences reflect discrimination rather than some neutral factor (*Mecklenberg* v. *Montana State Board of Regents* 1976).

Individual Plaintiffs and Judicial Deference

In a manner similar to early cases litigated under Title VII in which faculty members challenged negative decisions regarding promotion, tenure, or renewal, plaintiffs in early salary discrimination cases against colleges and universities seldom prevailed. Two trends are evident in early salary discrimination cases, whether litigated under Title VII, the Equal Pay Act, or both: Courts interpreted the "equal work" requirement strictly, and judges were exceedingly deferential to the judgments of academics as to exactly what salary an individual faculty member should command.

The inequality between the jobs compared in *Shipley* v. *Fisk University* [8 Empl. Prac. Dec. 9538 (M.D. Tenn. 1973)] resulted in defeat of the plaintiff's equal pay claim. The Dean of Women claimed that Fisk's Dean of Men was given rent-free quarters while she was not, although they had comparable responsibilities. The court, ruling for Fisk, found that the apartment was given to the Dean of Men in return for his directing the residence hall, an additional responsibility. The court made no serious attempt to determine why the Dean of Women had not been offered a similar opportunity to direct a residence hall in return for free accommodations; its review was limited to an analysis of the job each dean actually performed.

Similarly, a female faculty plaintiff suing under the Equal Pay Act lost when the court found that the male colleague with which she had compared her qualifications had four more years of experience than she [*Spieldoch* v. *Maryville College,* 13 Fair Empl. Prac. Cases 660 (E.D. Mo. 1975)]. Similarly, the equal pay claim of a female medical school faculty member was rebuffed when the court found that the "comparable" male faculty had more responsibility and taught more courses than did the plaintiff [*Molthan* v. *Temple University,* 442 F. Supp. 448 (E.D. Pa. 1977)]. In each of these cases, the courts looked only at the duties actually performed by the plaintiffs or their objective qualifications rather than at decisions about hiring or job assignments for indications of discrimination.

The sophistication of academic salary discrimination was advanced, to a degree at least, by the trial and appellate court opinions in *Keyes* v. *Lenoir Rhyne College* [15 Fair Empl. Prac. Cases 914 (W.D.N.C. 1976), *aff'd,* 552 F.2d 579 (4th Cir. 1977), *cert. denied,* 434 U.S. 904 (1977)]. Professor Annie Laurie Keyes alleged that the defendant college systematically discriminated against women faculty in decisions about hiring, promotion, and salary. The plaintiff attempted to prove the salary and employment discrimination by demonstrating the disproportionate hiring of male faculty and the significantly lower salaries paid overall to female faculty. The statistical evidence upon which the judge relied in finding for the defendant college is interesting when compared with more recent (and more complicated) salary discrimination cases. The college submitted data describing the ordinal rank of the highest salaried female faculty member at the college over a seven-year period; that rank ranged from first to fourteenth. The judge concluded that if one woman professor was the highest paid faculty member at the college, then the college did not discriminate against women. In addition, the court was impressed with the fact that Lenoir Rhyne College had a greater proportion of women faculty than the national average of women faculty across institu-

ions of higher education. The court thus found that each
discrepancy in pay and promotions of male and female
faculty was "based upon legal and logical reasons and not
upon sex" (p. 918).

The court in *Keyes* made it clear that judicial review of
academic salary and promotion decisions was an inappropriate role for the judiciary.

> *The standards set by Colleges and Universities as to*
> *qualifications for employment and promotion and*
> *salaries and benefits of faculty members are matters*
> *of professional judgment and [the] court should be slow*
> *to substitute its judgment for the rational and well-*
> *considered judgment of those possessing expertise in the*
> *field. How can the court evaluate the relative merit as to*
> *salary of a doctorate degree in Physics compared to a*
> *doctorate degree in Divinity?* (p. 924).

The result in *Keyes,* and perhaps in the other cases described in this section, may be attributed to a number of
causes, among which may be insufficient evidence to prove
a case of salary discrimination. The limited use of statistics, combined with the substantial deference of the *Keyes*
courts to subjective academic judgments, however, resulted in victory for the college in each case. Later cases,
where classes of plaintiffs used more sophisticated statistical tools to demonstrate systematic bias in salaries paid to
women, have resulted in victories for class plaintiffs and
have required defendant colleges to make substantial
adjustments in back pay and salary to its women faculty
and administrators.

Class Plaintiffs and Judicial Scrutiny

Just as judicial scrutiny has increased in academic litigation
over hiring, promotion, tenure, and renewal since the mid-
1970s, so has judicial scrutiny of academic salary discrimination cases. Recent class actions by women faculty
alleging discrimination in employment and compensation
have been more successful, with the exception of *Wilkens,*
which is still in litigation [*Wilkens* v. *University of Houston,* 654 F.2d 388 (5th Cir. 1981)], and *Sobel* [*Sobel* v.
Yeshiva University, 566 F. Supp. 1166 (S.D.N.Y. 1983)].

Each of the cases is interesting and instructive with regard to the degree of the court's willingness to compare faculty qualifications and the role played by the trial court judge in fashioning a remedy. None, however, ranged as far or had the potential to transform governance and decision making to the degree found in *Mecklenberg* (1976).

The elements of *Mecklenberg* related to Montana State University's practices regarding promotion and tenure were discussed in the previous chapter. The plaintiffs in *Mecklenberg* also claimed, however, that salaries paid to female faculty were consistently lower than those paid to comparable males. The plaintiffs' expert witness had performed a regression analysis, controlling for department, years of experience, and type of degree held. Rank was not included in the regression analysis because rank may be linked to discrimination in promotion practices. The court explained that, had rank also been held constant, the statistical effect of slower promotions for women faculty (which the court found to be true at Montana State) would have been ignored (p. 6496). The results of the regression analysis showed that it would require nearly $250,000 to equalize salaries for women (p. 6496).

The university defended the substantial differences in salaries and the general underrepresentation of women by asserting that women did not apply to Montana State because of its climate and its geographical isolation; it also claimed that promotions were less frequent for women faculty because their careers were slowed by family obligations. The university could provide no data to support these claims, however, and the trial judge gave them no credence, calling them "totally speculative" (p. 6494).

The remedy resulting from the *Mecklenberg* case is significant because of its breadth and because of the manner in which it was developed. The judge ordered the parties not only to reach a negotiated settlement for the adjustment of back pay and salaries but also to jointly develop a revised governance process (including decision making on hiring, promotion, and tenure) so that the systemic problems that led initially to the discrimination could be corrected by faculty and administrators themselves (Clark 1977). A joint faculty-administration team developed recommendations for salary adjustments, based on pairing,[8] and women were added to the membership of all governance and personnel committees. Procedures for making all decisions related to employment—hiring, promotion, tenure, and salary—were developed and implemented. No decision before or since *Mecklenberg* has required such substantial changes in decision-making processes at a university. The university did not appeal the decision, nor have subsequent federal trial courts relied upon *Mecklenberg*'s approach or remedy. Its value as precedent is therefore questionable.

The next major salary discrimination case in higher education, *Marshall* v. *Memphis State University,* also concerned a university whose salary decisions were nonstandardized and decentralized.[9] The approach used by the judge in the *Memphis State* case differed substantially from the *Mecklenberg* court's approach, however. In *Memphis State,* the Department of Labor had investigated salary practices at the university and alleged that 42 present or former female faculty members were paid less than their male colleagues in 17 departments. The department demonstrated the underrepresentation of women at high faculty and administrative ranks and argued that, as in *Mecklenberg,* the system itself was permitted to perpetuate discrimination against women because there were no systemic safeguards to prevent it (LaNoue 1982, pp. 21– 22). The university's defense was to attack the qualifications of the female plaintiffs and to assert the need for department chairs and deans to make subjective judgments about faculty using flexible criteria.

Unlike the judge in *Mecklenberg,* the trial judge in *Memphis State* did not believe it necessary to order modifications in the university's decision-making procedures or criteria. He stated that employment decisions concerning college faculty were necessarily subjective,

[8]In pairing, a female faculty member is "matched" to a male faculty member in the same discipline with the same degree, number of years of experience, and other objective criteria, and their salaries are compared. Although pairing permits objective comparisons between persons of similar qualifications, it is not completely effective because it is often difficult to find a male faculty member whose job and qualifications are similar enough to permit the comparison.

Because this 1980 decision is unpublished, the discussion relies upon a description of the case by one of the trial experts involved in the litigation (LaNoue 1982).

apparently believing that a systemic remedy was unnecessary. The judge did, however, decide to examine the salary pairs offered as evidence by the Department of Labor. According to LaNoue, "Judge Welford found himself considering the relative value of a medieval English specialist versus other specialists in an English department, [and] whether teaching public administration involved the same skill, effort and responsibility as teaching political science. . ." and ordered salary adjustments and back pay for 27 female faculty members (LaNoue 1982, p. 24).

Despite the similarity of the plaintiffs' claims in *Mecklenberg* and *Memphis State* that institutionwide changes in decision-making processes were necessary, the only similarity in outcome is that pairing was used to ascertain the amounts of salary adjustments necessary. LaNoue emphasizes that the approach taken by the trial court judge in these and other cases is the least predictable and most significant factor affecting the precise outcome of the case (if the plaintiffs prevail) and the remedy ordered (LaNoue 1982). Clearly, differences in judicial approach affected the outcome in a case decided shortly after *Memphis State, Marshall* v. *Georgia Southwestern College* [489 F. Supp. 1322 (M.D. Ga. 1980)].

The case against Georgia Southwestern College (GSC), also brought by the Department of Labor, concerned alleged violations of the Equal Pay Act in the salary levels of female faculty members. As was the case in *Mecklenberg* and *Memphis State,* salary determinations were decentralized and made on the basis of flexible and often unarticulated criteria. The court found that at GSC, women tended to be paid less because there was "a greater supply of prospective female faculty members and a willingness of females to accept lower beginning salaries" (p. 1326). The court noted that salary increases were usually a percentage of current salary, resulting in increasingly wider gaps between men's and women's salaries with each successive year.

The judge ruled that the skill, effort, and responsibility required of all faculty were equal, obviating the need for the individual comparisons performed by the judge in *Memphis State* (p. 1326). Therefore, the judge found, GSC had violated the Equal Pay Act because of an "overall subjective system which results in men generally being paid more than women." He also found sex discrimination in the salary decisions for six specific women faculty (pp. 1327–29). (The Department of Labor paired the six women with six male colleagues in the same discipline on the basis of highest degree, number of years at GSC, number of years since obtaining the doctorate, and teaching ability, and showed the women's salaries to be substantially lower in each case.) The defendant college used a "marketplace" defense, alleging that salary determinations were made based upon the "market worth" of the faculty member. The judge refused to accept such a defense:

> [A]ny credibility that the market force defense might have is diminished by the fact that those charged with hiring did not inform themselves of the market rates of particular expertise, experience or skills. The hiring process is devoid of any bargaining over initial salaries, a process one would normally expect in the context of a competing market (p. 1331).

The judge ordered three years of back pay for the six plaintiffs and suggested that he would consider ordering that the salary structure of the entire public college and university system in Georgia be overhauled and rationalized, somewhat like a Civil Service salary system, with salary grades and step increases within grades (p. 1325). He suggested that such a standardized system would be preferable to the decentralized, arbitrary method of determining salaries used by the college. The trial court decision is on appeal; to date no "civil service" system has been implemented for Georgia's public college and university faculty (LaNoue 1982, p. 26).

While the issues in *Mecklenberg, Memphis State,* and *Georgia Southwestern College* are similar, virtually the only similarity in terms of the conduct of the litigation was the use of pairing to make comparisons between "similar" men and women faculty. Pairing is an imperfect tool at best, however, for even if a "match" can be found for a female faculty member (and often one cannot be found), comparing two individuals on a number of dimensions can never be completely objective. How does one compare two otherwise "similar" faculty when one published a re-

[S]alary determinations were decentralized and made on the basis of flexible and often unarticulated criteria.

spected scholarly book and the other won a teaching award (Koch 1982, p. 12)? Although research suggests that matching a national sample of faculty pairs can overcome some of the problems of comparability (Koch 1982, p. 12), such comparisons have not been used extensively in litigation involving academic salary discrimination.

A more sophisticated statistical tool, multiple regression, has been used in at least two recent academic salary discrimination cases. Although the outcome of each case differed, it is useful to examine both how the court viewed the validity of regression analysis as a probative device and the variables used by the parties to arrive at predicted salaries for female faculty.

Judicial Reception of Regression Analysis

The statistical tool of multiple regression is useful for studying the variables affecting faculty salary levels because it permits a quantitative estimate to be made about the effect of a variety of independent variables upon a dependent variable—salary. The independent variables that are believed to explain salary variance are used to develop a "predicted" salary for an individual, based on that person's individual characteristics concerning that variable (for example, highest degree held, number of years of experience). Predicted salaries and actual salaries are then compared for the individuals alleging salary discrimination (Fisher 1980; Greenfield 1977, pp. 50–51).

For the regression analysis to be probative and useful as a tool to discover any effects of discrimination, however, the variables used as "predictor" variables (independent variables) cannot themselves be linked to discrimination, or the resulting regression analysis will not accurately reflect the degree of discrimination. For example, experts have argued that rank may be a "tainted" variable because promotion may be decided in a discriminatory manner or may be influenced by impermissible or illegal criteria (Finkelstein 1980; Koch 1982, p. 12). Thus, regression analysis must be planned carefully and evaluated cautiously before conclusions are drawn. Several researchers have investigated this topic in depth, and their concerns about the variables chosen for the regression should be given careful consideration (Koch 1982; Pezzullo and Brittingham 1979).

The need for careful design and interpretation of regression analyses was evident in a recent case tried in the Fifth Circuit. Although the plaintiffs in *Wilkens* v. *University of Houston* (1981) have not yet prevailed, the court endorsed the use of regression analysis as a tool to ferret out alleged salary discrimination.[10] The plaintiffs, two nonteaching professionals, sued under Title VII, claiming that the university systematically discriminated against women in hiring, promotions, and salaries. Because the regression analysis introduced by the plaintiffs did not control for the academic discipline of the faculty members (for example, law or engineering versus the social sciences), the court found the statistics flawed and unconvincing. The university also introduced two multiple regression analyses of faculty salaries into evidence. The first analysis used eight factors that explained 52.4 percent of the differential between men and women; the second added sex as a ninth factor and explained 53.2 percent of the variation, a difference of less than 1 percent (p. 403). Although it appears that several of the variables used in the university's regression were correlated with sex and thus "tainted" variables (for example, experience as a full professor, department, possession of a doctorate other than a Ph.D.), the plaintiffs did not introduce expert testimony to challenge the variables employed by the university's regression analysis. The court, seemingly annoyed with the flaws in both statistical analyses, declared:

> Multiple regression is a relatively sophisticated means of determining the effects that a number of different factors have on a particular variable; while it may be the best, if not the only, means of proving classwide discrimination with respect to compensation in a case such as this . . . it is subject to misuse and thus must be employed with great care. Ideally, when a multiple regression analysis is used, it will be the subject of expert testimony and knowledgeable cross examination from both sides. In this manner, the validity of the model and the signifi-

[10]The plaintiffs lost their case at both the federal trial and appellate court levels. They successfully appealed to the Supreme Court on a procedural matter, however, and the case has been remanded to the trial court for further findings.

*cance of its results will be fully developed at trial,
allowing the trial judge to make an informed decision as
to the probative value of the analysis . . . (p. 403).*

The court thus sanctioned a new theory of academic salary
discrimination litigation, where expert witnesses would
prepare and defend regression analyses of faculty salary
data, leaving the judge to determine the credibility of each
expert and the validity of each regression technique used.

Such an event came to pass in a recent salary discrimination case against the City University of New York
(CUNY) system [*Melani* v. *Board of Higher Education,
City of New York,* 561 F. Supp. 769 (S.D.N.Y. 1983)]. The
class plaintiffs, all female members of the "professional
instruction staff" at CUNY, alleged that sex discrimination
influenced "virtually all facets of [the] defendant's employment practices including hiring, promotion, salary, and
fringe benefits (p. 772). The plaintiffs, who sued under Title
VII and Section 1981 of the Civil Rights Act, presented
statistical evidence as their entire case, relying on two
regression analyses performed by a trial expert (a labor
economist). The first study analyzed the salaries of all
CUNY employees between 1972 and 1977; it also analyzed
separately the salaries of persons hired after 1972 (the year
that Title VII first became applicable to colleges and
universities). The first study grouped faculty by highest
degree, age, years of service for CUNY, and years since
obtaining the highest degree, using a modified pairing
method (p. 775). The second study performed a multiple
regression analysis on the data used in the first study and
other data, resulting in an analysis of 98 independent
variables. This large number of variables included mea-
surements of the quality of an academic degree (for example, an R.N. versus a C.P.A.), time elapsed between each
degree acquired, and a number of objective characteristics
of faculty (p. 776). Sex was also included as an independent variable. The analysis performed on both the entire
staff and the subset of post-1972 hires found sizable salary
differentials between men and women that were statistically significant (p. 776).

The defendant Board of Higher Education attacked the
validity of the pairing technique because it "matched"
males and females on as few as two characteristics. The

court agreed with the board's allegation, asserting that the first study "fail[ed] to control for multiple influences on salary" (p. 777); it ruled that, without more evidence, the first study would have been insufficient to establish a prima facie case of salary discrimination. Although the defendant also asserted that the regression analysis excluded relevant explanatory variables and treated people with dissimilar responsibilities as comparable, the trial judge found the analysis to be sufficiently probative to establish a prima facie case of sex discrimination, noting that the defendant had not successfully demonstrated the inaccuracy or insignificance of the regression analysis (p. 781). Although the defendant board offered a statistical report purporting to justify the salary discrepancies, the judge found the defendant's statistical evidence "fatally flawed" (p. 782). While a remedy has not yet been ordered in *Melani,* the plaintiffs' attorneys estimate that salary adjustments and back pay awards could exceed $60 million (McFadden 1983).

Approximately three months after the *Melani* opinion was announced, however, a different trial judge in the same federal district court ruled in favor of a university in an equal pay case. Female doctors employed at Yeshiva University's Albert Einstein College of Medicine alleged that the university discriminated against all full-time women faculty at the medical college in both salary and pensions (*Sobel* v. *Yeshiva University* 1983). As in *Wilkens* and *Melani,* both the plaintiffs and the defendant college hired experts to run regression analyses on selected data regarding faculty characteristics and their effect upon salary levels.

The *Sobel* opinion chronicles the difficulties and disputes among experts for both sides in determining which variables were appropriate to include in the regression analyses. For example, the relevance of information concerning a faculty member's administrative responsibilities, emphasis on clinical work or research, location of the medical school from which the degree was earned, and the type of medical specialty practiced (for example, pediatrics versus neurosurgery) was disputed. The court criticized the plaintiffs' experts for failing to include variables in the regression analyses that could have been responsible for salary differences, including quality of research, quality of teaching, significance of publications, grant procurement, and the significance of a faculty member's "contributions to science" (p. 166). The court found these variables, and others not measured by the plaintiffs' experts, to have a significant influence on individual salaries, declaring that "the failure to adequately account for productivity resulted in an underadjustment bias and plaintiffs' overstatement of the sex coefficients" (p. 166). Furthermore, the court agreed that several variables used in the plaintiffs' regression were collinear (they measured the same phenomenon and thus were not independent) (p. 167). Because the court found the plaintiffs' statistical analysis unreliable and because no "anecdotal evidence" (testimony about specific acts of discrimination, for example) was available to the court, the judge ruled that the plaintiffs had not proven a prima facie case of sex discrimination, and he dismissed the case.

Although *Sobel* involved a battle among statistical experts, as did *Wilkens,* the trial judge's attitude in *Sobel* toward the validity of statistics in salary discrimination cases was less sanguine than the comments of the judge in *Wilkens.*

> *Mark Twain supposedly once said that there are three kinds of lies: lies, damned lies, and statistics. Though perhaps hyperbolic, this declaration of distrust aptly warns that any conclusion based on statistics may be unsound* (p. 156).

Despite the judge's apparant antagonism toward reliance upon statistical proof in litigation involving discrimination in employment, his analysis of the complicated evidentiary issues and disputes was thorough and demonstrated some understanding of the technique and its limitations.

The willingness of trial judges to accept and evaluate the probative value of regression analyses, combined with the size of the damage awards for which colleges and universities are potentially liable, suggests that issues of salary equity may pose greater threats of litigation to higher education than any other single issue. The issues are complicated and the evidentiary requirements technical and ill defined. The outcome of a few cases suggests that some courts may view a civil service–type of salary scale as the only kind of compelling objective salary policy that the Equal Pay Act seems to require. Despite the complexity of the issues in these cases and their similarity in many respects, litigation outcomes have been variable and often only loosely related to the issues in the case. Thus, in developing guidelines for administrative practice, the most useful analysis will be a summary of judicial review, the range of outcomes, and the actual evidence found useful by the trial courts.

One facet of the recent salary discrimination litigation is troublesome and could present substantial problems to future defendant colleges. Despite the relatively large number of scholarly articles addressing the use of regression analysis in academic salary litigation, unanswered questions persist. How can the parties, and especially the judge, be certain that only relevant variables have been used? How well do the variables measure important faculty characteristics (such as teaching effectiveness or scholarly productivity)? Can we really say with confidence that *all* unexplained variance is a result of sex discrimination? How can these statistical tests be made more useful? These questions are especially important because judges, not experts in statistical analysis, are deciding whether a particular regression analysis "proves" or "disproves" salary discrimination. One wonders if the tool, at least as it has been used thus far, merits such judicial confidence.

Summary
Despite the fact that both Title VII and the Equal Pay Act are very specific in the burdens of proof required of both parties and the extent of the remedies available, the approach of the trial judges in the various cases has varied widely.[11] The judge in *Mecklenberg* examined the entire governance system at Montana State University, while the judge in *Memphis State* considered individual salaries and did not address systemic issues. The trial judges in *Wilkens* and *Melani* focused upon the variables used in the regression analysis and virtually ignored the manner in which salaries were decided. Clearly, some of the differences in

[11]Title VII limits back pay to two years; the Equal Pay Act normally limits back pay to two years but permits a third year if the court finds the violation to have been "willful."

the scope of judicial review may be related to variations in the way plaintiffs presented their cases and the evidence that plaintiffs relied upon. Much of the difference among these cases, however, appears to be attributable to the individual views of the trial judges involved toward the appropriate judicial scope of review (LaNoue 1982), which is unfortunate because it makes it difficult for both plaintiffs and defendant colleges to plan a strategy for litigation or to predict which claims might be most successful.

Such individuality in judicial approach is also evident when the range of remedies ordered in academic salary discrimination cases is analyzed. Remedies have ranged from salary adjustments for fewer than half the litigants in *Memphis State* to a negotiated institutionwide salary settlement in *Mecklenberg* to a potentially statewide reformation of public college and university salary practices in *Georgia Southwestern College*. The remedies in *Wilkens* and *Melani* are yet to be determined. This uncertainty is especially troublesome to administrators who may be faced with the decision of whether to settle or go through with the litigation. Indeed, one university, attempting to head off litigation by women faculty, established salary minima for women faculty. The university found itself in court anyway when 92 male faculty who were paid less than comparable females sued under the Equal Pay Act and prevailed [*Board of Regents, University of Nebraska* v. *Dawes,* 522 F.2d 380 (8th Cir. 1975), *cert. denied,* 96 S. Ct. 1112 (1976)]. It would seem that college administrators lose either way: Litigation is costly and damages could be in the millions of dollars, while some attempts to ameliorate prior salary discrimination can actually engender litigation. The cases do suggest an approach to salary determinations, however, that can not only aid colleges in defending lawsuits but could also lead to fairer decisions in the bargain.

Although later cases have tended to view all faculty jobs as requiring the same "skill, effort, and responsibility," this issue is debatable and arguments can be made for making distinctions among faculty. Heading an academic program, organizing service activities for a department, serving on important and time-consuming governance committees, among other activities, can serve as valid criteria for distinctions in salary. A valid merit pay system based upon clearly articulated criteria exempts salary determinations from the Equal Pay Act. Accurate and complete data on the "market value" of individuals with degrees in certain disciplines may justify discrepancies in the salaries paid to various otherwise "comparable" faculty members. In other words, the courts have not said that distinctions may not be made among seemingly comparable faculty but only that these distinctions must be carefully documented with well-supported reasons.

This report has so far focused upon areas of employment law that have been extensively litigated and upon laws whose intent is reasonably well understood. While not designed specifically for employees of colleges and universities, both laws are, after a decade of litigation and development of judicial precedent, applied quite routinely to employment disputes in academe.

Unfortunately, such a history of clarification and stable interpretation is not the case for a law designed specifically for academe that was passed the same year Title VII and the Equal Pay Act were applied to higher education. From its passage in 1972, Title IX has engendered dispute over its intent, the scope of its coverage, the meaning of some of its operative language, and the nature of its remedies. In particular, considerable dispute has raged over whether Title IX protects employees of colleges and universities, as well as students, from sex discrimination. This chapter describes the law's provisions and analyzes its legislative history and regulations as the primary clues to the intent of Congress regarding the application of Title IX to discrimination in employment. It then analyzes several recent federal cases in which the scope of Title IX has been defined. Finally, the chapter briefly describes regulations establishing a college's responsibilities under Title IX, noting their implications for faculty and administrative conduct.

The Controversy

Title IX of the Education Amendments of 1972 states:

No person in the United States shall, on the basis of sex, be excluded from participation in, be denied the benefits of, or be subjected to discrimination under any educational program or activity receiving Federal financial assistance [20 U.S.C. §1681(a)].

The law clearly covers discrimination on the basis of sex in any educational organization's programs or activities receiving federal financial assistance. Any federal agency dispersing federal money to educational organizations was required to write regulations to implement the law. The literature and case law have focused primarily on regulations promulgated by the Department of Education [34

C.F.R. §§106.1–106.71 (1980)] as a substantial proportion of federal aid to education is dispersed by that department. The Department of Education's basic assumption in developing the regulations was that Title IX prohibits sex discrimination against students and employees of an educational organization.

Courts were reluctant to include employment within the provisions of the regulations throughout most of the 1970s. [See, for example, *Seattle University* v. *HEW,* 621 F.2d 992 9th Cir. 1980), *vacated sub nom United States Department of Education* v. *Seattle University,* 102 S. Ct. 2264 (1982); *Romeo Community Schools* v. *HEW,* 600 F.2d 581 (6th Cir. 1979), *cert. denied,* 444 U.S. 972 (1979); *University of Toledo* v. *HEW,* 464 F. Supp. 693 (N.D. Ohio 1979). In light of the *North Haven* decision, *infra,* the Supreme Court vacated and remanded both the *Seattle University* case and the *Dougherty* case, *infra.*] Therefore, the literature contains only limited discussions of the issue of Title IX in employment. For example, Hendrickson and Mangum (1977) discuss Title IX as a new tort, emphasizing implications for athletics and admissions. Given the precedent of legal decisions, it appears that the then Department of Health, Education, and Welfare (HEW) and later the Department of Education had exceeded the authority of the statute in writing regulations concerning sex discrimination in employment.

Two cases in the Second and Fifth Circuits, however, would change this previously unanimous interpretation of the scope of Title IX. *North Haven Board of Education* v. *Hufstedler* [629 F.2d 773 (2d Cir. 1980)], using an extensive analysis of the legislative history, found that congressional intent concerning the scope of Title IX included employment within educational institutions receiving federal funds. The Fifth Circuit, in *Dougherty County School System* v. *Harris* [622 F.2d 735 (5th Cir. 1980), *vacated sub nom Bell* v. *Dougherty County School System,* 102 S. Ct. 2264 (1982)], while finding that Title IX covered employment, limited the coverage to those programs where employees' compensation was provided wholly or in part by federal funds. These two cases served to raise the issue and move it toward a decision by the Supreme Court. They also resulted in an increase in the number of articles concerned with the issues of Title IX and employment

From its passage in 1972, Title IX has engendered dispute over its intent, [its] scope . . . and . . . its remedies.

(see, for example, *Brooklyn Law Review* 1981; Murphy 1981; Salomone 1979; *University of Pennsylvania Law Review* 1980).

Two key issues face the Court (*Michigan Law Review* 1980). The first concerns what makes an institution a "recipient" of federal financial assistance. Federal aid to institutions can take the form of direct grants or loans to the institution or indirect grants or loans to students. Does only direct federal aid constitute a recipient, or does any federal aid make the institution a recipient? The second issue concerns whether Title IX covers only those programs within the institution that receive federal financial assistance or whether receiving any form of federal aid brings the entire institution under the proscriptions of Title IX.

This chapter reviews the issue of employment under Title IX as recently outlined by the Supreme Court. The issues cited above are also presented in light of recent and pending decisions. To understand these decisions, it is appropriate first to review the legislative history and post-legislative review of Title IX regulations.

Legislative History and Regulatory Review
The legislative history of Title IX becomes the key to determining whether Congress intended the title to cover employment. Most courts found the review of congressional intent unclear as to the statute's coverage. In *North Haven* v. *Hufstedler* (1980), however, the Second Circuit looked not only at the debate during passage of Title IX but also at Congress's actions following enactment, including a congressional review of HEW's proposed regulations for Title IX. By using this analysis, the court found that the scope of Title IX includes employment. While including actions after enactment was a somewhat new approach for determining legislative intent, the Supreme Court would use the same analysis on appeal.

When reviewing debate during the passage of Title IX, the court analyzed debate recorded in the *Congressional Record*. In this particular instance, evidence regarding intent centers around the comments of Senator Bayh, who proposed the amendment and offered prepared comments on the day of passage in the Senate. The court quoted Senator Bayh's statement in proposing the amendment:

*Amendment No. 874 is broad, but basically it closes
loopholes in existing legislation relating to general
education programs and employment resulting from
those programs. . . . [T]he heart of this amendment is a
provision banning sex discrimination in educational
programs receiving Federal funds. The amendment
would cover such crucial aspects as admissions procedures, scholarship, and* faculty employment, *with limited
exceptions. Enforcement powers include fund termination provisions—and appropriate safeguards—parallel to
those found in Title VI of the 1964 Civil Rights Act.
Other important provisions in the amendment would
extend the equal employment opportunities provisions of
Title VII of the 1964 Civil Rights Act to educational
institutions, and extend the Equal Pay for Equal Work
Act to include executives, administrative and professional women* [118 *Cong. Rec.* (1972), p. 5803, emphasis
added].

While Senator Bayh's statements at the time of presenta-
tion of the amendment are instructive, comments during
final debate before passage are more instructive. In re-
sponse to a question from Senator Pell about the scope of
Title IX, Senator Bayh said:

*. . .As the Senator knows, we are dealing with three
basically different types of discrimination here. We are
dealing with discrimination in admission to an institution, discrimination of available services or studies
within an institution once students are admitted, and
discrimination in* employment *within an institution, as a
member of a faculty or whatever* [118 *Cong. Rec.* (1972),
p. 5812, emphasis added].

In a determination of legislative intent, the comments of
one senator are not controlling. As the author of the
legislation, however, Senator Bayh provides an important
guide to congressional intent, as the Supreme Court
pointed out in *North Haven Board of Education* v. *Bell*
[456 U.S. 512 (1982)].

The debate in the House of Representatives is scant and
contains little on Title IX. What does exist, however,

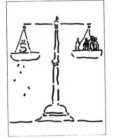

indicates that the House version of the amendments used language similar to that in the Senate [117 *Cong. Rec.* (1971), p. 39263], suggesting that Congress intended Title IX to cover employment.

The history of the legislation after enactment lends additional support to the premise that Title IX was intended to cover employment. HEW submitted proposed regulations on Title IX in June 1974. Those regulations (39 *Federal Register* 22228) included Subpart E, which contained prohibitions for discrimination in employment based on sex. The department received 10,000 comments on Title IX (Salomone 1980, p. 436). Under the provision of congressional review [20 U.S.C. §1232 (d)(1) (1974)], Congress has 45 days from the time an agency publishes proposed regulations to enact a legislative veto of the regulations, either as a whole or in part. Three resolutions were presented to Congress objecting to the provisions covering employment in the Title IX regulations (Salomone 1979). Two of them were concurrent resolutions presented by Congressmen Quie and Erlenborn. The other, a resolution by Senator Helms, was an attempt to veto the entire set of regulations. Congress passed none of the resolutions. The courts cited the lapse of time, four years, between enactment of Title IX and the regulatory review as weakening the importance of this information in showing legislative intent. It does, however, add additional weight to the premise that Title IX involves employment (Salomone 1979).

Finally, Senator Helms attempted in 1975 to limit Title IX's coverage of employment, but no action was taken on the bill [121 *Cong. Rec.* (1975), pp. 23845–47]. In 1976, Senator McClure presented an amendment to the 1976 Education Amendments that would restrict Title IX to "curriculum or graduation requirements of institutions. . ." [122 *Cong. Rec.* (1976), p. 28136], but the amendment was not approved.

Congressional actions after enactment should not be given the same weight as the legislative history. The Supreme Court stated in *North Haven* v. *Bell,* however:

> *Although postenactment developments cannot be accorded "the weight of contemporary legislative history, we would be remiss if we ignored these authori-*

*tative expressions concerning the scope and purpose of
Title IX . . ."* [Cannon v. University of Chicago *441 U.S.
at 687, n 7]. Where "an agency's statutory construction
has been 'fully brought to the attention of the public and
the Congress,' and the latter has not sought to alter that
interpretation, although it has amended the statute in
other respects, then presumably the legislative intent has
been correctly discerned". . . (North Haven v. Bell
1982, p. 519).*

Title IX Cases

The key case under Title IX employment issues is *North
Haven* v. *Bell* (1982). At issue before the Supreme Court
was whether Congress intended Title IX to cover sex
discrimination in employment at institutions receiving
federal financial assistance. The case involved the consoli-
dation of two cases from the Second Circuit involving the
North Haven Board of Education and the Turnbull Board
of Education [629 F.2d 773 (2d Cir. 1980)]. Both boards of
education maintained that the Department of Education
and previously the Department of Health, Education, and
Welfare had exceeded their authority in drafting Subpart E
of the regulations on Title IX covering employment discrimination. Using an analysis similar to that discussed
previously, the Court reviewed the legislative history and
postenactment history of Title IX. It found that employment discrimination comes within the prohibitions of Title
IX, upholding the conclusion of the Second Circuit.

The Court, however, may have narrowed the scope of
Title IX by reinterpreting the program-specific nature of
the statute. In disagreeing with the Second Circuit, the
Court noted that the act addressed sex discrimination in
programs receiving federal financial assistance.

*Title IX's legislative history corroborates its general
program-specificity. Congress failed to adopt proposals
that would have prohibited* all *discriminatory practices
of an institution that receives federal funds. . . . In
contrast, Senator Bayh indicated that his 1972 amendment, which in large part was ultimately adopted, was
program-specific. . . . Finally, we note that language in
§§601 and 602 of Title VI, virtually identical to that in
§§901 and 902 and on which Title IX was modeled, has*

been interpreted as being program-specific. . . . We
conclude, then, that an agency's authority under Title
IX, both to promulgate regulations and to terminate
funds, is subject to the program-specific limitations of
§§901 and 902 (North Haven v. Bell 1982, p. 519).

As this case involved a review of summary judgment as to
the agency's authority to write regulations, the facts of the
case did not allow the Court to define further what a
program is or what type of federal aid is necessary to
become a "program receiving federal financial assistance."
Neither did the Court decide whether sex discrimination
existed in these situations. That issue was remanded to the
district court for determination on the facts. Therefore,
subsequent case law must address questions of the definition of a "program" and what constitutes "federal financial
assistance."

The ruling in *North Haven* v. *Bell* may have narrowed
the scope of Title IX because of that part of the opinion
dealing with program specificity. A good example of this
narrowing effect was a case in Virginia [*University of
Richmond* v. *Bell,* 543 F. Supp. 321 (E.D. Va. 1982)]. The
University of Richmond, a private institution, asked for
injunctive and declaratory relief to stop an impending
investigation of its athletic programs by the Department of
Education. The Department of Education's Office of Civil
Rights based its authority to investigate the institution's
athletic programs on the receipt of a $1,900 federal grant
for library resources, maintaining the grant brought the
institution within the ambit of Title IX. The university
maintained that its athletic programs received no financial
assistance from the federal government. The question is
whether Title IX and its regulations have an "institutional
scope," as maintained by the Office of Civil Rights, or
whether they apply only to those programs receiving direct
federal financial assistance. Relying on the holding in
North Haven v. *Bell,* the district court found that the
athletic department did not receive federal financial
assistance and therefore was not subject to Title IX. While
acknowledging that the meaning of federal financial assistance is yet to be interpreted, this court interprets *North
Haven* v. *Bell* as narrowing the scope of Title IX regula-

tions to include only those programs that receive specific federal financial assistance.

Another example of the narrowing of the scope of Title IX is *Bennett* v. *West Texas State University* [525 F. Supp. 77 (N.D. Tex. 1981)]. Six West Texas State University students brought suit, alleging that the university had discriminated against women and denied them access to intercollegiate athletics. The university argued that its athletic programs did not come under the jurisdiction of Title IX because the athletic programs did not receive federal financial assistance. The court found the regulations on Title IX invalid to the extent that they apply to the whole institution rather than specific programs receiving federal financial assistance. Therefore, the court reasoned, unless the program in which discrimination was alleged to have occurred received financial assistance from the federal government, it does not come under the ambit of Title IX. The court did not accept the argument that the athletic programs benefit indirectly because the institution's receipt of federal funds makes other institutional funds available to the athletic program. Such "indirect benefit" was insufficient, the court believed, to require the application of Title IX to the athletic program.

While these cases indicate a narrowing of Title IX, several more recent cases appear to broaden its scope. The key case now before the Supreme Court (Docket No. 82–792) is *Grove City College* v. *Bell* [687 F.2d 684 (3d Cir. 1982), *cert. granted*, 51 U.S.L.W. 3611 (Feb. 22, 1983)]. Students brought suit against the Department of Education because the department had withdrawn Pell Grants and Guaranteed Student Loan monies after Grove City College had refused to file an assurance of compliance in accordance with the regulations for Title IX. The district court held that Title IX regulations were invalid and granted summary judgment to Grove City College, preventing the termination of federal financial aid. The Department of Education appealed, and the case was reviewed by the Third Circuit Court of Appeals, which reversed the lower court decision.

The Third Circuit addressed the question of whether indirect financial aid in the form of Pell Grants and Guaranteed Student Loans (both of which are awarded to *stu-*

dents, not to colleges) constituted federal financial assistance within the meaning of Title IX. Citing the ruling in *North Haven* v. *Bell* regarding the program specificity of Title IX, the court stated:

> . . . *[W]e believe that Congress intended that full scope be given to the nondiscriminatory purpose that Title IX was enacted to achieve, and that the program-specific terms of Title IX must therefore be construed realistically and flexibly. By so doing, contrary to Grove's argument, complete accommodation can be achieved between the concepts of "indirect federal financial assistance" and "program-specific" requirements* (*Grove City* v. *Bell* 1982, p. 697).

Therefore, the Third Circuit said, indirect financial aid to students is federal financial aid within the meaning of the law. Further, the court defined the meaning of "program," ruling that because the federal money flowing into the institution was not earmarked for specific programs and thus benefited all facets of the institution, the institution became a program under the meaning of Title IX.

> *Where the federal government furnishes indirect or nonearmarked aid to an institution, it is apparent to us that the institution itself must be the "program." Were it otherwise, and if it had to be demonstrated that each individual component of an integrated educational institution had in fact received the particular monies for a particular purpose, no termination sanction could ever effectively be imposed* (*Grove City* v. *Bell* 1982, p. 700).

Thus, the court ruled, Grove City College was a program under the meaning of Title IX because it received "nonearmarked aid" through federal student financial aid programs.

Another case decided by the Third Circuit following *Grove City* was *Haffer* v. *Temple University* [688 F.2d 14 (3d Cir. 1982)]. Temple University students sued the institution, alleging discrimination on the basis of sex in their athletic programs. The institution argued that its athletic programs did not receive federal financial assistance and therefore were not subject to Title IX. The Third Circuit followed its ruling in *Grove City* v. *Bell* and ruled that the athletic programs did receive federal financial assistance in the same way as Grove City College, through its students' Basic Educational Opportunity Grant funds, therefore becoming a program receiving federal financial assistance. The university's receiving federal financial assistance through federal student financial aid programs makes the athletic programs subject to the requirements of Title IX. Summary judgment was denied and the case went back to the lower court for a decision on the merits.

The *Haffer* and *Grove City* cases relied heavily on a previous case [*Bob Jones University* v. *Johnson*, 396 F. Supp. 597 (D.S.C. 1974), *aff'd mem.*, 529 F.2d 514 (4th Cir. 1975)]. Comparing the legislative history of Title VI to the issue under Title IX, the court ruled that a recipient of federal funds includes an institution that receives federal scholarship monies from students. While it is possible that the Supreme Court, when it considers *Grove City* v. *Bell*, may rule consistent with the judge in *Bob Jones University* v. *Johnson*, the outcome is uncertain, and such an interpretation of "recipient" may be inconsistent with congressional intent.

> *[T]he court ruled that a recipient of federal funds includes an institution that receives federal scholarship monies from students.*

Although legislative history suggests Congress disfavored applying Title VI to indirect funding, it also shows that Congress contemplated more than a simple direct/indirect test for identifying Title VI and Title IX recipients. The executive and legislative branches envisioned a distinction between "ultimate beneficiaries" and "recipients" of federal assistance. Congress drafted both statutes to protect ultimate beneficiaries from misconduct by recipients, and intended their sanctions to apply only to recipients—not beneficiaries. "Ultimate beneficiaries" of federal funds are those intended to reap the benefits of the aid. Students are the ultimate beneficiaries of most federal programs aiding education. "Recipients" should be defined as those institutions that receive federal funds and have discretionary power to disburse or spend them to aid these ultimate beneficiaries (Michigan Law Review 1980, p. 615).

The purpose of the act, in other words, is to "prevent discrimination against beneficiaries, not to restrict the use of federal aid by beneficiaries" (p. 620). Discussions during congressional debate may have taken place to ensure that federal funds were not to be used to promote discrimination but that beneficiaries were not to lose necessary funds (p. 620). Based on this balancing between the prevention of discrimination and the protection of beneficiaries from unnecessary hardship, the author proposes the use of the infection theory.

> ... *Rather than assume that all aid will be terminated or that only aid to the smallest identifiable discriminating unit must be cut, courts and agencies should balance the degree of discriminatory infection in each department or school against the extent of hardship that cutoffs would inflict on the division's student beneficiaries* ... (p. 624).

The use of "infection theory" may be just the middle ground the Supreme Court is looking for.

The question of how the Supreme Court will interpret the meaning of "recipient" and "program" under Title IX is soon to be answered. Whether the Court finds that a recipient is any institution receiving direct or indirect aid and is therefore a program under the title, or whether a recipient is only those areas of the institution receiving direct financial aid is mere conjecture at this point. There is at least a 50 percent chance that *Grove City* v. *Bell* could be followed and that institutions as "recipients" of federal student financial aid would therefore be programs under the meaning of Title IX.

Adjudication and Remedies
The cases discussed all deal with the question of the jurisdiction and scope of Title IX. None of these cases, however, yield answers to how a court would conduct an adjudication on the merits. Administrative remedies are available under Title IX where discrimination occurs. A complaint could be filed with the Department of Education's Office of Civil Rights or with the federal agency from which the institution received federal funds. (The Office of

Civil Rights is the agency used most often.) After the complaint is filed, the investigating agency sends a letter of finding to the institution where probable discrimination is found. Should the institution fail to rectify the problems identified in the letter of finding, it could lose federal funds.

Title IX also allows for the right of private action as clarified in *Cannon* v. *the University of Chicago* [648 F.2d 1104 (7th Cir. 1981), *cert. denied*, 454 U.S. 811 (1981)], referred to as *Cannon II*. *Cannon II* seems to indicate that a plaintiff need not exhaust the administrative remedies under Title IX to have standing to litigate.

Some questions on adjudication on the merits remain unanswered, however. How would a plaintiff demonstrate that discrimination has occurred? What must the defendant do to counter allegations of illegal employment practices? *Cannon II* is the only case available that deals with the merits of a Title IX suit. This case was heard on remand from the Supreme Court decision in *Cannon I* [*Cannon* v. *the University of Chicago*, 441 U.S. 677 (1979)], which established the private right of action in a Title IX case.

In *Cannon II,* the Seventh Circuit dealt with the question of whether the "disparate impact" standard used under Title VII or the intentional discrimination standard required under Title VI should apply to cases brought under Title IX. The court, noting the drastic nature of cutting off federal funds, stated:

> In short, we believe that a majority of the Justices on the Supreme Court as well as other courts that have recently addressed this question in similar circumstances would hold that a violation of Title VI requires an intentional discriminatory act and that disparate impact alone is not sufficient to establish a violation. We shall therefore adopt that standard under Title IX and evaluate appellant's complaint accordingly (*Cannon II* 1981, p. 1109).

The court further noted that an intent to discriminate cannot be shown simply by "a mere failure to equalize an apparent disparate impact" (p. 1110). Therefore, the plaintiff will have to show that the institution intended to discriminate and cannot rely solely on the discriminatory prove intent in a Title IX employment case. This ruling could make the institution's defense under Title IX close to insurmountable for a plaintiff.

Finally, the question of remedies should the plaintiff win remains elusive. Other Title IX cases not involving employment indicate that injunctive relief and attorneys' fees would be awarded, but punitive damages would not be allowed. In *Lieberman* v. *University of Chicago* [660 F.2d 1185 (7th Cir. 1981), *cert. denied,* 102 S. Ct. 1993 (1982)], the court stated:

> *[F]urthermore in light of the private right of action for injunctive relief authorized by* Cannon I, *coupled with provisions for an award of attorney's fees contained in 42 U.S.C. §1988, a grieved individual has at least one effective means of enforcement. . . . If a damages remedy should be created, it should be fashioned by Congress, not by the courts* (p. 1188).

Whether employment discrimination under Title IX will follow the cases involving admissions, such as *Lieberman* v. *University of Chicago,* remains to be seen. Certainly one could fall back on cases involving Title VI of the Civil Rights Act of 1964, as the Title IX regulations make Title VI enforcement procedures applicable to Title IX (*Procedures,* Subpart F, §106.71). Title VI employment cases may be different, however, because a plaintiff may be required to show a defendant's intent to discriminate, rather than the more easily proven discriminatory impact, to establish a violation under Title VI. This issue is before the Supreme Court in *Guardian Association of New York City Police Department* v. *Civil Service Commission of the City of New York* [633 F.2d 233 (2d Cir. 1980), *cert. granted,* 51 U.S.L.W. 3547 (Jan. 11, 1982)]. Therefore, while it is difficult to speculate, given the current case law, remedies at a minimum should include attorneys' fees and injunctive relief. Damages in the form of back pay seem plausible, but the issue is speculative at this point.

Title IX Regulations
While the courts are still interpreting the meaning of "program," "federal financial assistance," and "recipi-

ent," it is important to be aware of the regulations (34 C.F.R. §§106 *et seq.*) for those units within an institution that clearly come under Title IX because they are funded with federal monies. The regulations specifically covering employment are in Subpart E. Section 106.51 states that the regulations cover employment criteria, recruitment procedures, hiring and promotion, compensation, job assignments, collective bargaining agreements, leaves, fringe benefits, marital and parental status, training and apprenticeship programs, employee-sponsored recreational and social activities, and other employment privileges for program recipients of federal financial assistance.

Employment criteria (§106.52) cover tests or other criteria used in employment. These tests or criteria must not have an adverse effect on individuals of one sex unless they can be shown to "predict valid successful perform- ance" or alternative tests or criteria are not available. The section covering recruitment procedures (§106.53) pro- hibits discrimination in recruitment. Where employers have been found to have discriminated during recruitment in the past, they must rectify the situation by recruiting members of the sex that was discriminated against. This section also prohibits use of organizations that furnish prospective employees who are "predominantly" or "exclusively" of one sex.

With regard to compensation (§106.54), a "recipient" may not make distinctions in pay or other compensation for equal work on the job based on sex, may not classify jobs for one sex, or may not maintain separate promotion or tenure systems. The section on fringe benefits (§106.56) prohibits an employer from granting fringe benefits based on sex. Fringe benefits must be equal in both contributions and the awarding of benefits.

Marital or parental status (§106.57) protects an employee from actions by the employer based on "potential marital status or family status." An employer may not treat individuals differently based on whether they are the head of a household. Further, a recipient may not discriminate against an individual based on her pregnancy and must treat pregnancy as a temporary disability that will not affect her status, fringe benefits, seniority, or any other benefits offered employees. If pregnancy leave is not available, the employer must treat pregnancy as a leave of absence without pay, resulting in a guarantee to the employee of no loss of seniority gained before the leave.

Section 106.58 negates any state law that would require a recipient of federal funds to limit employment to one sex. The recipient must also provide benefits mandated by the state for one sex to members of the other sex in its employ.

A recipient of federal financial assistance may not discriminate or show preference in advertising (§106.59) for a job. The prospective employer who is a recipient may not inquire about the marital status or sex of a prospective employee (§106.60). Sex as a job qualification can be used only where it can be shown to be a bona fide criterion for successful performance of a particular task (§106.61)—rest room attendants, for example.

Employers who are recipients of federal financial assistance need to be aware of these regulations. The regulations should be measured against current policies and practices and appropriate changes implemented. Faculty directing research projects using federal funds should be made aware of these provisions before they begin hiring research assistants.

Summary

It is clear since the Supreme Court's ruling in *North Haven* v. *Bell* that Title IX covers employment. What remains unsettled, however, is whether an entire institution or only those programs receiving federal aid fall under Title IX's requirements. The Court will soon define a "recipient" of federal financial support in *Grove City* v. *Bell,* determining whether indirect federal financial aid in the form of student loans and grants makes the entire institution a "recipient" and therefore a "program" subject to the proscriptions of Title IX. Whether the Court takes this broad approach or the narrow approach that only direct federal financial aid defines a program has serious implications for enforcement of Title IX and for future litigation against colleges and universities.

FINANCIAL EXIGENCY AND MANDATORY RETIREMENT

The solution to the economic crisis at some institutions is a declaration of financial exigency, necessitating the removal of tenured faculty. Even the 1940 policy statement on academic freedom and tenure published by the American Association of University Professors (1977) recognizes financial exigency as a rationale for reducing staff. The AAUP Bulletin (1974) provides some operating guidelines for institutions involved in the termination of tenured faculty under financial exigency. While termination for cause usually involves the faculty member's personal conduct (Gray 1981) and charges of a personal nature require the use of due process procedures to protect the person's good name from unjustified defamation, termination resulting from disability, elimination of a program, financial exigency, or mandatory retirement does not involve reasons reflecting on a person's conduct or reputation and therefore does not necessitate the same level of procedures (Mingle 1981, p. 73).

While termination for disability or program elimination is not covered in this chapter, it is clear that institutions' boards of trustees are empowered by law to establish programs consistent with the institution's charter and mission. They therefore are empowered to eliminate degree programs that are inconsistent with that charter and mission. While trustees clearly have the legal right to terminate programs and to lay off tenured faculty, the wisest course in reducing or eliminating programs is to ensure the equitable treatment of affected faculty and rudimentary due process (especially in public institutions). After examining the legal issues surrounding the reduction or elimination of programs, Olswang (1982–83) concludes that case law does not require across-the-board or seniority-related reductions unless institutional rules or a collective bargaining agreement requires them (pp. 436–37).[12]

[12]College administrators should also consider the contractual rights of students. Case law indicates that this contractual right may require an institution to phase out a program gradually unless it can show "an impossibility of performance" in the current situation (Olswang, Cole, and Wilson 1982). Courts have awarded damages under certain circumstances when a breach of contract with students has occurred as a result of eliminating a program. While this report is concerned with faculty employment in the event of financial exigency, administrators should be aware of possible legal implications involving currently enrolled students.

This chapter discusses the case law on financial exigencies and institutional prerogatives and obligations to faculty. Institutions anticipating retrenchment may rely heavily on anticipated retirements to reduce staff as an alternative to laying off tenured faculty. The Age Discrimination in Employment Act of 1967 (ADEA), which raises the mandatory retirement age, therefore takes on added significance. To understand the nature of the legal requirements of financial exigencies, it is first necessary to understand the nature of the tenure contract.[13]

The Nature of a Tenure Contract
Tenure is an unintegrated, unilateral, lifetime employment contract. "Unintegrated" means that not everything is spelled out in the contract document but that other documents (for example, the faculty handbook, college catalog, or board of trustees bylaws and minutes) are considered as part of the contract (*Iowa Law Review* 1976, p. 488). "Unilateral" means that one party agrees to the expressed terms of the contract without gaining an "expressed promise or performance" from the other party (*Black's Law Dictionary* 1979, p. 294). The university offers lifetime employment without defining specific tasks to be performed by faculty members, leaving them great freedom in fulfilling their responsibilities for teaching and research.

Because the "contract" is unilateral and a formal written document signed by both parties does not always exist, there is some question as to whether a contract really exists. The doctrine of consideration is used to prove the existence of the tenure contract if the following formal functions are present: (1) tenure is granted either through written notification or through notation in official minutes; (2) the decision is made after a probationary period, based on deliberate evaluation of past performance as a teacher and researcher; (3) the institution's functions of learning and research necessitate this type of contractual relationship to further society's interests; (4) the institution's

---

[13]The issue of financial exigency is much more complex than the issues with which the courts have dealt. While these issues are beyond the scope of this chapter, administrators may find it helpful to consult Hample (1981) and Mingle (1981) for guidance in dealing with financial exigencies. Both publications emphasize planning strategies for dealing with retrenchment and the reduction of staff.

policies indicate that a decision about tenure is one requiring serious deliberation and is one made with the expectation that it will be long term (*Iowa Law Review* 1976, pp. 499–500). These provisions are consistent with the purposes of the tenure contract and serve to validate its existence in a court of law.

In private institutions, the written tenure contract, other institutional documents, and previous practices govern the rights of tenured faculty in cases where a breach of the contract has been alleged. "The legal effect of a tenure system is to place restrictions on the power of the employing institutions to terminate tenured professors except for cause after a hearing" (Brown 1977, p. 280). A definition of cause and the procedures for the hearing are spelled out in the contract or implied through accepted institutional procedures.

Public institutions, on the contrary, are governed not only by the contract but also by the constitutional prerogatives of the Fourteenth Amendment. The original Bill of Rights deals with a citizen in his relationship with the federal government. The Fourteenth Amendment applies those guarantees to citizens in their relationship with state government. That amendment forbids a state from making any laws that infringe on the protection of a person's equal rights under the law or deprive an individual of rights without the due process of law. Public institutions, as agents of state government, must guarantee those rights to citizens. One of the rights guaranteed is an individual's property rights, created either by law or by contract. A job possessed through a contract or with a reasonable expectation of reemployment is viewed as property. The Fourteenth Amendment mandates the use of due process procedures if a person is denied his property (a job) (Gray 1981, p. 173).

Two cases decided in the Supreme Court clearly require procedural due process at a public institution where a property interest in the job exists because of an existing implied or written tenure contract [*Perry* v. *Sinderman*, 408 U.S. 593 (1972)] or where other constitutional freedoms (such as freedom of speech) may be infringed upon as a result of the removal of a nontenured or tenured faculty member [*Board of Regents* v. *Roth*, 408 U.S. 564 (1972)]. "Proof of such a property interest would not, of course, entitle [the faculty member] to reinstatement. But such proof would obligate college officials to grant a hearing at his request, where he could be informed of the grounds for his nonretention and challenge their sufficiency" (*Perry* v. *Sinderman* 1972, p. 603).

Clearly, then, public institutions are strictly required to provide due process in the removal of tenured faculty. When faculty are removed by reason of financial exigency, however, the requirement for due process is somewhat less.

Financial Exigency: The Accepted Prerogative

The courts have honored contracts or institutional policy specifically stating that shortage of funds (financial exigency) allows the termination of tenured contracts [*AAUP* v. *Bloomfield College*, 136 N.J. Super 442, 346 A.2d 615 (App. Div. (1975); *Scheuer* v. *Creighton University*, 199 Neb. 618, 260 N.W. 2d 595 (1977)] and have upheld the institution's prerogative to dismiss tenured faculty. Many institutions have not specifically stated in the tenure contract that financial exigency is a basis for removal of tenured faculty, however; instead, they have formally adopted or accepted in a published document the AAUP standards governing tenure.

> *After the expiration of a probationary period, teachers . . . should have permanent or continuous tenure, and their service should be terminated only for adequate cause, except in the case of retirement for age, or under extraordinary circumstances because of financial exigency.*
> *Termination of a continuous appointment because of financial exigency should be demonstrably* bona fide (American Association of University Professors 1974).

If this document is incorporated into the contract, financial exigency as a cause for dismissal becomes a part of the contract [*Browzin* v. *Catholic University of America*, 527 F.2d 843 (D.C. Cir. 1975)].

If financial exigency is neither directly nor indirectly mentioned in the contract or supporting documents, the courts have ruled that the prerogative exists because it is common academic practice. In *Krotkoff* v. *Goucher*

College [585 F.2d 675 (4th Cir. 1978)], the court cited the
AAUP 1940 policy statement on tenure:

> The reported cases support the conclusion that tenure is
> not generally understood to preclude demonstrably bona
> fide *dismissal for financial reasons. . . . In other words,
> where the contract did not mention this term [financial
> exigency], the courts construed tenure as implicitly
> granting colleges the right to make* bona fide *dismissals
> for financial reasons* (p. 679). [See also *Browzin* v.
> *Catholic University* 1975 and *Johnson* v. *Board of
> Regents of the University of Wisconsin System, 377* F.
> Supp. 227 (W.D. Wisc. 1974), *aff'd,* 510 F.2d 975 (7th
> Cir. 1975).]

Because the rationale for financial exigency has become
part of accepted academic standards in higher education, it
is a legal prerogative in laying off tenured faculty. In those
cases where an institution has already incorporated specific
policies or guidelines on financial exigency in its employment contracts or other relevant documents, however, the
courts have applied the institution's policy rather than the
AAUP guidelines.

Case Law on Financial Exigency

The case law on financial exigency presented here com-
prises primarily federal cases on the issue. This section
explains the courts' interpretation of defining a bona fide
financial exigency, identifying the appropriate decision
makers, defining appropriate criteria, clarifying due
process procedures, defining good faith and the burden of
proof, describing the liability issue, and terminating an
existing annual contract.

Defining a bona fide financial exigency

The courts have defined an appropriate financial exigency
as an existing deficit in an institution's operating budget
(*AAUP* v. *Bloomfield College* 1975; *Krotkoff* v. *Goucher
College* 1978), and they have held that legislative reductions in an operating budget constitute a bona fide financial
exigency [*Brenna* v. *Southern Colorado State College*, 589
F.2d 475 (10th Cir. 1978); *Johnson* v. *Board of Regents*

*The courts
have honored
contracts . . .
specifically
stating that
shortage of
funds . . .
allows the
termination of
tenured
contracts. . . .*

1974; *Klein* v. *the Board of Higher Education of the City of New York,* 434 F. Supp. 1113 (S.D.N.Y. 1977)]. They have also held that the financial exigency need not exist in the institution as a whole but rather can be limited to a single academic unit, such as a college or department (*Brenna* v. *Southern Colorado State College* 1978). In *Scheuer* v. *Creighton University* (1977), the court stated:

> We specifically hold the term "financial exigency" as used in the contract of employment herein may be limited to financial exigency in a department or college. It is not restricted to one existing in the institution as a whole (p. 601).

Krotkoff v. *Goucher College* (1978) clearly establishes that an institution does not have to liquidate capital and assets before declaring a financial exigency. An institution may not, however, remove 13 tenured faculty and replace them with 12 new faculty, as was done at Bloomfield College (*AAUP* v. *Bloomfield College* 1975). Declining enrollment can be used to justify the existence of a financial exigency and the removal of a specific faculty member (*Brenna* v. *Southern Colorado State College* 1978); *Krotkoff* v. *Goucher College* 1978).

Identifying appropriate decision makers

The second issue is to identify who is authorized to develop and implement the criteria for laying off faculty if a financial exigency exists. Every case reviewed recognizes that the board of trustees or the equivalent body has the clear authority to make such decisions. It is also apparent from the case law that the board may delegate that authority to the president [*Johnson* v. *Board of Regents* 1974; *Klein* v. *the Board of Higher Education* 1977; *Grany* v. *Board of Regents of the University of Wisconsin System,* 92 Wisc. 2d 745, 286 N.W. 2d 138 (1979)]. General guidelines developed by the board for the president or others to use in making decisions about laying off faculty were present in most of the cases reviewed. In some cases, department heads or deans were qualified to select faculty to be laid off, so long as they stayed within the general guidelines (*Brenna* v. *Southern Colorado State College* 1978; *Krotkoff* v. *Goucher College* 1978). In most of the cases, the recommendations regarding layoffs were also supported by recommendations of faculty study committees organized to evaluate and recommend appropriate action [see, for example, *AAUP* v. *Bloomfield College* 1975; *Brenna* v. *Southern Colorado State College* 1978; *Krotkoff* v. *Goucher College* 1978).

Defining appropriate criteria

The third issue is to define the appropriate criteria for selecting faculty to be laid off because of financial exigency. The cases indicate that nontenured faculty should in most cases be selected first and that tenured faculty must be given the opportunity to fill vacant positions for which they are qualified. Certainly, declining enrollments can be used as a basis for selecting programs where faculty can be cut. The courts also say, however, that the administration or board has discretionary power to decide who will be cut when a financial exigency exists, so long as the decision is not arbitrary and capricious (see, for example, *Johnson* v. *Board of Regents* 1974).

The case law also indicates that seniority need not be used as the overriding criterion for deciding who will be laid off. In *Krotkoff* v. *Goucher College* (1978), a tenured faculty member with more seniority was selected for removal before a younger faculty member, because the younger faculty member had the qualifications to meet the college's curricular needs more effectively. In *Brenna* v. *Southern Colorado State College* (1978), a nontenured faculty member of a two-faculty department was retained instead of the tenured faculty member. The reason given was that the nontenured faculty member gave the department more flexibility in making teaching assignments because the tenured faculty member had stated that he was not qualified to teach courses other than those he was currently teaching.

The employer's use of criteria, such as competency as a teacher or researcher, as the basis of a decision to remove a tenured faculty member because of a financial exigency, however, would implicate the faculty member's liberty interest under the Fourteenth Amendment. Such use would mandate a hearing before the layoff to ensure due process (see, for example, *Perry* v. *Sinderman* 1972 and *Board of Regents* v. *Roth* 1972). The rationale for this is that the ability to find employment elsewhere may be in jeopardy, thus requiring greater precautions to prevent unfair or unjustified damage to one's reputation. The requirement for due process would be less strict for a financial exigency if no reference to a person's competency is part of the reason for dismissal, because courts have believed that mere termination for a neutral reason does not affect future employment opportunities or tarnish a person's reputation. Choosing faculty on the basis of an individual's qualifications to perform certain tasks is appropriate and within administrative discretion.

Clarifying due process procedures

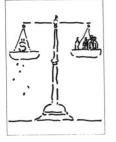

Because the tenured faculty member at a public institution who is laid off because of financial exigency is being denied a property interest (his job), the Fourteenth Amendment is implicated. The requirements for due process under financial exigency as mandated by the courts have been less exacting than those mandated for a faculty member removed for cause (for example, incompetence or moral turpitude). In *Johnson* v. *Board of Regents* (1974), the court outlined the specific requirements necessary to meet the tenured faculty member's rights to due process:

> *1. Furnishing each plaintiff with a reasonably adequate written statement of the basis for the initial decision to lay off;*
> *2. Furnishing each plaintiff with a reasonably adequate description of the manner in which the initial decision had been arrived at;*
> *3. Making a reasonably adequate disclosure to each plaintiff of the information and data upon which decision makers had relied; and*
> *4. Providing each plaintiff the opportunity to respond* (p. 240).

After identifying the faculty who were targeted for layoff, the University of Wisconsin unit chancellors selected faculty to serve on a "reconsideration committee." The committee was to review the faculty member's appeal of the decision and might (but was not required to) agree to meet with the faculty member. This meeting was not to be adversarial, nor was the university required to prove its position; its purpose was rather to allow the faculty time to show why the university's rationale should not be followed or to correct erroneous information. The court stated that the reconsideration committee should determine whether evidence was sufficient to support the decision and to ensure that the procedures spelled out by the system had been followed. The court also ruled that the unit chancellor could make the initial decisions about layoffs, appoint the faculty to serve on the reconsideration committee, and make the final decision about layoff without violating the faculty member's rights to due process. In support of these procedures, the court cited *Arnett* v. *Kennedy* [416 U.S. 134 (1974)], a Supreme Court case in which these procedures were applied to a layoff where permanence was attached to employment. Other cases have followed these standards; thus, *Johnson* v. *Board of Regents* (1974) suggests an appropriate due process in the dismissal of tenured faculty when financial exigencies exist [see also *Brenna* v. *Southern Colorado State College* 1978; *Bignall* v. *North Idaho College,* 538 F.2d 243 (9th Cir. 1976); *Klein* v. *the Board of Higher Education* 1977; *Krotkoff* v. *Goucher College* 1978; *Jiminez* v. *Almondovar,* 650 F.2d 363 (1st Cir. 1981)].

Defining good faith and the burden of proof

The key to a decision by the courts in a case of financial exigency is whether the institution has exhibited good faith in the decision to terminate faculty. *AAUP* v. *Bloomfield College* (1975) provides an explication of a court's view of "bad faith." The institution's attempt to hire new faculty a year after tenured faculty were terminated because of a financial exigency, its decision to rescind tenure for *all* faculty members, and what appeared to the court to be ex post facto policy pronouncements by the board of trustees to justify the terminations were evidence to the court that the college acted in "bad faith." Good faith, in contrast, is indicated by an attempt to find other positions for dismissed faculty members, the existence of a bona fide financial exigency, reasonable standards for making decisions about faculty members' dismissal, and the fair application of those standards (Gray 1980, p. 396). Further, the institution must prove that it acted in good faith (see *AAUP* v. *Bloomfield College* 1975; *Browsin* v. *Catholic University* 1975; *Krotkoff* v. *Goucher College* 1978), and the standards for meeting the burden of proof are the same as the standards defining good faith (Gray 1980, p. 399).

Some plaintiffs have claimed that a college's refusal to retrain them for a different job was evidence of the college's bad faith. In *Krotkoff* v. *Goucher College* (1978), for example, the plaintiff stated that the college should pay for retraining to permit the French professor to teach economics, which would have required a doctorate in economics. The court disagreed.

Describing the liability issue

In *Grany* v. *Board of Regents* (1979), a group of terminated faculty of the University of Wisconsin system sued the Board of Regents for damages. The court ruled that the doctrine of sovereign immunity prevented state officials, acting in the normal role of their office, from being sued. Damage claims could be brought (in Wisconsin), however, against the individual for "negligent performance of ministerial duties" (p. 144). The court ruled that the dismissals were within the officials' discretion, were conducted under procedures that did not deny faculty protections owed them, and were not arbitrary dismissals for personal reasons. There were no other allegations of "malicious, willful, or intentional misconduct by board members" (p. 149), and the suit was therefore dismissed.

Personal liability claims could arise in financial exigency cases if a faculty member could show that the decision was arbitrary, that the decision was made for reasons other than those stated, or that procedural rights were denied. A claim could also be supported if it could be shown that the faculty member's constitutional rights at a public institution had been violated. The Supreme Court held in *Wood* v. *Strickland* [420 U.S. 308 (1975)] that a civil claim for damages could be possible if a public official were to deny an individual his rights under the Constitution. Ignorance of those rights was no defense against a claim for liability. The "qualified good faith" immunity that *Wood* v. *Strickland* applied to administrative behavior, however, suggests that only the most blatant violations of constitutional rights would expose administrators to liability.

Terminating an existing annual contract

The question remains as to whether an institution because of financial exigencies could terminate an employee who has a contract for a specific period within the period covered by the contract. In *Karr* v. *the Board of Trustees of Michigan State University* [325 N.W. 2d 605 (Mich. App. 1982)], Michigan State attempted to lay off an employee for several days because of financial exigency, thereby reducing his annual salary. The university argued that in the interest of public policy a contract stating a specific payment for services or a fixed period should not be enforced in the face of a financial exigency. The Michigan Court of Appeals found, however, that no authority existed to breach either an existing contract for a fixed term or guaranteed payment of a certain sum because of a financial exigency. The court believed that because the contract existed, it must be honored. The court stated that honoring a binding contract would aid the university in acquiring and holding qualified faculty and therefore would actually promote sound public policy, thus negating the institution's argument. It would appear that financial exigencies will not be accepted as an excuse to alter or terminate the conditions contained in a contract for a fixed period or for an exact sum. Administrators should recognize that state, not federal, law governs contracts. Thus, while some states may permit colleges to execute binding term contracts containing an "escape clause" that would render the contract unenforceable in the event of financial exigency, a precedent has already been established in Michigan that negates such a law.

The clear trend in litigation permits a college undergoing a financial crisis to terminate tenured faculty. The courts accord broad discretion to college administrators to develop procedures for selecting programs to reduce or eliminate and to select faculty to be laid off. As long as the standards developed for layoffs are uniformly applied and the fiscal crisis is provable, the courts will generally require no more of a college.

While financial exigency may legally be easier than retirement to use to reduce staff, using such procedures may result in the youngest faculty members' being laid off. Aging faculty may therefore have the greatest protection, even though some are less productive than some junior

---

faculty members. The next section describes the legal limitations on colleges' and universities' retirement policies.

Age Discrimination
Reductions in staff created by retirements will help institutions balance reduced budgets. The Age Discrimination in Employment Act (ADEA) [29 U.S.C. §§621–34 (1981)], however, raises the mandatory retirement age from 65 to 70. That change could significantly affect colleges and universities.

Until July 1, 1982, higher education was exempt from mandatory retirement at age 70. Professors who can retire later mean an aging staff and perhaps adverse effects on the institution's budget.

> *For higher education, age 70 retirement almost certainly means an older professoriate that in turn poses a management dilemma: how to maintain the teaching and research effectiveness of an older faculty and what to do about younger instructors. There are already too many young instructors for available tenure positions. To resolve this dilemma, the college or university may have to institute benefit plan revisions, new evaluation procedures, career and preretirement planning, and flexible work arrangements—all of which may have an adverse effect on the campus budget* (Foster 1981, p. 16).

The impact of ADEA is felt in other areas. The law prohibits discrimination on the basis of age for employees 40 to 70, and it covers any benefits given or policies governing employees, including hiring, promotion, compensation, and other benefits.

This section reviews the legislation pending in Congress, the fundamental questions currently before the Supreme Court challenging congressional authority to regulate retirement policies for state employees, case law dealing with ADEA, and the impact of the law on various institutional policies.

Current congressional action
Three bills are currently before Congress. Senate Bill 686 would eliminate any mandatory retirement age in ADEA

but would exempt postsecondary institutions, allowing them to maintain 65 as a mandatory retirement age. Senate Bill 832 would also remove any mandatory retirement age from ADEA but would exempt postsecondary institutions for 15 years, thereby allowing colleges and universities to maintain 70 as a mandatory retirement age. A companion bill to S. 832, H.R. 2161, is before the House of Representatives. At least one House staff employee predicts S. 686 will not pass but that S. 832 and H.R. 2161 will probably be enacted within the next year.[14] This state of flux adds to the difficulties of planning in higher education.

Congressional authority

The Supreme Court has decided a case that challenges the congressional authority to regulate state employees' retirement policies [*EEOC* v. *Wyoming,* 514 F. Supp. 595 (D. Wyo. 1981), 51 U.S.L.W. 4219 (March 2, 1983]. At issue was whether the Tenth Amendment limits congressional authority to regulate state employees or whether the amendment is limited by Article I, Section 8 of the U.S. Constitution, the so-called "Commerce Clause." The Tenth Amendment reserves certain powers to state government, which may include state employer-employee relationships, while the Commerce Clause allows the federal government to regulate interstate commerce subject to constitutional limitations. In *EEOC* v. *Wyoming,* the state alleged that ADEA as applied to state employees violated the Tenth Amendment. The EEOC sued the state of Wyoming for discrimination on the basis of age in setting mandatory retirement for law enforcement officials at 55. The district court found that *National League of Cities* v. *Usery* [426 U.S. 833 (1976)] applied. In following *Usery,* the court held that the federal government's regulatory authority under the Commerce Clause must be found to loom larger as a national interest in eliminating discrimination than the state's authority to regulate its employees. The court saw the federal government's policy of age discrimination against foreign service and federal law enforcement employees as giving any argument of national interest a hollow ring. They found that ADEA did not

Professors who can retire later mean an aging staff and perhaps adverse effects on the institution's budget.

[14]Telephone interview with Steve McConnel of the House Select Committee on Aging, U.S. Congress, May 1983.

apply to game wardens because of the state's defined powers under the Tenth Amendment (*Usery* specifically covers police protection, sanitation, public health, and parks and recreation). As education is one of those powers traditionally viewed as being reserved to the states by the Tenth Amendment, it would appear that tenured faculty employed in state institutions would be insulated from ADEA if the Supreme Court were to follow the district court's findings in *EEOC* v. *Wyoming*. The key to the Court's decision hinges on the legislative history of the act. *National League of Cities* v. *Usery* (1976) involves the Fair Labor Standards Act of 1938 [29 U.S.C. §§201–19 (1976)] to which ADEA is linked, but ADEA is also linked to Title VII.

The Supreme Court, however, reversed the lower court's decision in *EEOC* v. *Wyoming,* stating that ". . . the purpose of the doctrine of immunity in *National League of Cities* [v. *Usery*] was to protect states from federal intrusion that might threaten their separate and independent existence . . ." (p. 4222). The Court cited *Hodel* v. *Virginia Surface Mining and Reclamation Assn., Inc.* [452 U.S. 264 (1981)], which summarizes a three-part test to determine whether a state should be immune from a particular federal statute. First, does "the challenged statute [regulate] the state as a state"? Second, does the federal statute cover areas that are "indisputably attrib-ute[s] of state sovereignty"? Third, does the federal law "impair [the state's] ability to structure integral operations in areas of traditional governmental functions"? (p. 4222). It was on this third point the Court found that ADEA does not impair the exercise of state government's attributes in regulating the retirement age of state game wardens. The Court argued that ADEA does not prohibit the state from setting a retirement age if it is a *"bona fide* qualification for the job of game warden" (p. 4223). The Court differenti-ated *Wyoming* from *Usery,* arguing that in *Usery* federal regulations would substantially affect the state's ability to allocate financial resources, while in *Wyoming* deferred retirement might save the state in other benefits paid because of early retirement. Therefore, "it will have either a direct or an obvious negative effect on state finances" (p. 4223). The other issue in *Usery* was that the federal

regulations inhibited the state's ability to use employees
"as a tool for pursuing social and economic policies
beyond their immediate managerial goals" (p. 4223), and
no such purpose was posited for retirement of game
wardens in *Wyoming*. The Court held that the extension of
ADEA to state employees was a valid exercise of congressional power "both on its face and applied to this case"
(p. 4224).

While the door may have slammed shut on any state
immunity from ADEA, the language of the decision does
not negate *National League of Cities* v. *Usery;* it simply
differentiates the federal Fair Labor Standards Act from
ADEA based on the impact on state governmental prerogatives. One cannot help but wonder if the Court would rule
the same way on the exemption of college or university
faculty. States may be able to argue that such limits on
mandatory retirement of faculty may substantially limit the
state's ability to chart the course of crucial educational and
research policies at their institutions, thus limiting a state's
prerogative if it is not allowed to retire nonproductive
scholars at a certain age to maintain the vitality of the
institution. The issue may never reach the Court, however,
as states absorb the ruling and adapt retirement policies.

Case law on ADEA
Several recent cases shed light on the types of issues one
can expect to see under ADEA. In *Leftwich* v. *Harris
Stowe State College* [540 F. Supp. 37 (E.D. Mo. 1982)], a
college formerly under the control of the St. Louis Board
of Education was transferred to the state college system.
In the process of the transfer, all positions were terminated
and applications taken to fill them. The 47-year-old plaintiff, having held tenure with the college when it was under
the control of the St. Louis Board of Education, applied
for a tenured associate professor position. He was not
hired and subsequently brought charges alleging that hiring
a 30-year-old nontenured person and a 62-year-old black
tenured faculty member for the two positions for which he
was qualified constituted discrimination on the basis of age
and race. The court found that the charge brought under
ADEA was valid as the institution's action of reserving
some positions for nontenured faculty had a disparate

impact on former tenured faculty over 40. The institution's rationale for its action, economic savings, was not a valid excuse to defend a prima facie case of disparate impact. The court also found that the institution violated Title VII and ordered the institution to hire the plaintiff. (This case should not be generalized to all institutions that choose to fund a nontenured position but applied to a unique situation comparable to *Leftwich* v. *Harris Stowe*.)

In *Sanders* v. *Duke University* [538 F. Supp. 1143 (M.D.N.C. 1982)], a 58-year-old medical professor filed suit alleging violations under ADEA in the awarding of salary adjustments, secretarial assistance, and fringe benefits. In *McCroan* v. *Bailey* [543 F. Supp. 1201 (S.D. Ga. 1982)], a 68-year-old bookstore clerk filed suit alleging discrimination under ADEA because her cashier's position had been downgraded to a part-time position. Although both of these cases were dismissed on procedural grounds, they demonstrate several areas of potential litigation under ADEA.

Finally, *Levine* v. *Fairleigh Dickinson University* [646 F.2d 825 (3d Cir. 1981)] indicated that the award of tenure can be separated from employment. Furthermore, separating tenure and employment is consistent with other case law. *Drans* v. *Providence College* [383 A.2d 1033 (R. I. 1978)], while not dealing with ADEA, ruled that an institution's policy establishing a mandatory retirement age did not breach a tenure contract between the professor and the institution because the contract was silent concerning retirement age. In *Levine* v. *Fairleigh Dickinson,* a 65-year-old faculty member lost his tenure status but continued employment under a one-year contract when the current ADEA legislation went into effect. Because he no longer had tenure when ADEA was enacted, he did not come under the exemption for higher education that was in effect through January 1982. ADEA therefore applied, and the court ruled that the professor's contract for the 1979–80 academic year could not be reduced from full-time to part-time status simply on the basis of his age. This case indicates that even when tenure and employment are separated at age 65, the faculty member will have a claim to employment through age 70 under ADEA. Institutions will apparently not be able to terminate a faculty member before age 70 without substantial cause.

ADEA regulations and employee benefits

Employers do not have to offer exactly the same retirement, pension, and insurance plans to all employees, but differences in benefits must be based on "actuarially significant cost considerations" (Foster 1981). For example, the amount of term life insurance provided for an older employee might be less than for a younger employee, because insurance rates increase with age. Benefits for older employees can be reduced using a "benefits package" approach, but the total cost of the package must not be less than what would be allowed in a benefit-by-benefit approach, and retirement and pension plans may not be included in the package. For benefits where age is not a cost factor, such as sick leave and paid vacations, workers cannot be treated differently based on age (Foster 1981). According to the regulations [29 C.F.R. §§1625.1 *et seq.* (1982)], employers may terminate contributions to retirement plans and benefit accruals at the normal retirement age. Finally, employers should review their benefit packages in light of the regulations to ensure they are in compliance with the law.[15]

Summary

Institutions of higher education facing reduced budgets will rely on financial exigencies as a reason to reduce staff. The courts have certified financial exigencies as a valid rationale for removing tenured faculty, but the institution has the burden of proving that the financial exigency exists and that it acted reasonably. Requirements for due process in public institutions necessitate a written statement on the basis for the decision, a description of the manner used in making the decision, disclosure of information and data used in making the decision, and an opportunity for the dismissed tenured faculty member to respond. One court also ruled that an institution may not breach a contract, negotiated either for a specific period or for a certain sum, during the contract period, even if financial exigency exists.

[15]In the summer of 1983, the U.S. Supreme Court ruled that Title VII prohibits sex-based differentials in pension benefits, even if such differentials are based on life expectancy. The Court ruled, however, that this precedent would be applied only prospectively [*Arizona Governing Committee* v. *Norris,* 103 S. Ct. 3492 (1983)].

ADEA will affect those institutions relying on retirements to mitigate the reduction of staff. The mandatory retirement age under the act of 70 necessitates institutions' planning in accordance with the regulations. Because the Supreme Court and Congress are both reviewing the act, the exact requirements are in a state of flux. Administrators may want to make contingency plans based on possible current changes.

SUGGESTIONS FOR ADMINISTRATORS

The number and complexity of the laws protecting faculty members' employment rights demonstrate the need for college administrators to understand the purposes of the laws and how the courts interpret them for academic institutions. Most importantly, administrators need to be aware of the procedures they should establish to protect faculty members' employment rights, both to ensure better employee relations and to avoid litigation.

It is equally important for administrators to avoid overreacting to the laws and their judicial interpretation. College and university administrators should recognize that, generally speaking, where courts have perceived a college's personnel procedures to be fair and have found that the college applied those procedures evenhandedly, courts have upheld the college's right to make and implement management decisions. In the relatively few cases in which faculty plaintiffs have prevailed, the courts have generally found the college's personnel practices to have been arbitrary or applied haphazardly.

It is . . . important for administrators to avoid overreacting to the laws and their judicial interpretation.

The following suggestions and guidelines therefore emphasize the development of good management practices as much as they emphasize compliance with the laws. This is not to say that fair employment procedures and equitable application of those procedures will shield a college from discrimination litigation, should discrimination occur. In fact, if colleges adopt the guidelines suggested herein, it will be more difficult for faculty or administrators to make discriminatory decisions, and frivolous lawsuits brought in situations where discrimination did *not* occur will be substantially easier for the college to defend.

This chapter first presents a series of general principles drawn from a wide range of academic employment litigation. Following these general guidelines is a series of recommendations for practice in specific situations (for example, denial of tenure or staff reduction during financial exigency). Throughout the chapter, it should be clear that neither the guidelines nor the cases from which they were developed require faculty or administrators to lower standards of performance or to settle for mediocre employees. The guidelines focus on equitable treatment and rationally developed procedures to buttress peer review and academic norms.

General Guidelines

It would be ludicrous to suggest that careful documentation of employment decisions and the development of uniform personnel procedures will eliminate discrimination from decision making. The following suggestions will, however, make it more difficult for a college to justify a purely discriminatory employment decision and, concomitantly, will make nondiscriminatory employment decisions easier to defend.

Data collection and record keeping

Throughout the lawsuits analyzed in this report, one indisputable theme has emerged. Colleges need to be able to justify the employment decisions they reach by clear data and careful documentation. In setting salaries, in making decisions about promotion or tenure, or in determining which faculty members will be laid off in the event of a fiscal crisis, it makes good managerial sense and provides a better litigating position if a college can clearly document its reasons for making a particular employment decision. The disinclination of courts to review the substance of the decision—only whether it was made fairly and supported adequately—provides further evidence of the wisdom of creating systematic data collection and record-keeping systems.

Uniform procedures

The court cases described in this report have, with considerable uniformity, refused to dictate the procedures to be used in making academic employment decisions. The courts *have* examined, however, the fairness of the procedures and whether they provided the affected employee an opportunity to learn the basis upon which the decision was made and, in some situations, an opportunity to appeal the decision. Administrators can protect their institutions by developing (with faculty advice) uniform procedures for hiring, promotion, tenure, and layoffs that are enforced by the institution and communicated to the affected faculty members.

This is not to say that all employment decisions must be standardized to the extent that music faculty are judged by the same standards as nuclear physicists. Peer review *criteria* may vary by discipline (as long as the nature of those criteria and their relative weights are disclosed to the affected faculty members), but the *procedures* for review should be uniform. And it is the responsibility of the administration to see that those procedures are enforced and are applied evenhandedly. Even in private colleges and universities where constitutional due process is not required, fair procedures should result in fairer decisions and, should litigation ensue, a stronger defense for the defendant college.

Faculty participation
It should be clear that the courts do *not* overturn academic employment decisions solely because of a lack of faculty members' participation in such decisions. In fact, the numerous statements of judicial deference to colleges' internal management decisions generally speak of superior administrative, not faculty, expertise. But including faculty in academic employment decisions makes good management sense for at least three reasons: (1) it results in better-informed decisions; (2) it enhances employee relations; and (3) it makes them less susceptible to reversal by the courts. The literature contains considerable support for the first and second reasons (Baldridge et al. 1978; Drucker 1980; Mortimer and McConnell 1978). The third reason is supported by the considerable deference with which courts regard peer review evaluations. Certainly, many colleges use peer review extensively for decisions about promotion and tenure—and about hiring as well. But decisions about salaries and staff reductions are frequently made without faculty participation, and employment decisions made by administrators may be more easily portrayed as arbitrary by a disaffected faculty member. While they have generally not required faculty participation in such decisions, the courts have viewed the use of peer review in employment decisions as evidence of administrative good faith [for example, in *Johnson* v. *Board of Regents of the University of Wisconsin System*, 377 F. Supp. 227 (W.D. Wisc. 1974), *aff'd*, 510 F.2d 975 (7th Cir. 1975)]. Nor does affording the faculty an opportunity to participate in employment decisions remove the decision from administrative discretion; the *Johnson* case itself demonstrates that a court will not require a university to comply with faculty recommendations. But using peer

review should result in better-informed employment decisions while it protects the decision, to a degree, from close judicial scrutiny.

Accountability for decisions

Fair procedures and well-supported decisions require accountability at every level of decision making. Each segment of the employment decision-making process should be able to document, in writing, the reasons for a positive or negative outcome. Strengths and weaknesses of the employees being evaluated should be stated clearly and documented carefully. If a negative decision is made on institutional grounds rather than because of an individual's deficiencies, the data for the institutional justification (for example, declining enrollment, shifting disciplinary emphasis, an excessive proportion of tenured faculty) should be collected and documented. This is not to say that the supporting data and justifications should necessarily be given to the employee in question but rather that the decision makers at every level should be held responsible for justifying their decision on the basis of clear evidence. A cautionary note is in order, however. Greater accountability does not lead inevitably to lowered standards or forced positive decisions about mediocre employees. It may, however, require some modifications in the way that departments handle probationary faculty, and it suggests that the productivity and performance of all employees should be evaluated and documented regularly.

Beyond the four general suggestions for overall employment practices, a number of specific suggestions have been developed from the laws and litigation described in previous chapters. Although the courts have not required all of the suggestions, implementing the suggestions should result in fairer and more easily documented employment decisions.

Hiring, Promotion, and Tenure

Employment practices for probationary faculty will become increasingly important as the number of new faculty positions declines and the number of tenure denials rises. The following suggestions should alert probationary faculty to the college's expectations for their productivity and performance, the criteria used to evaluate them, and how those criteria are weighted.

1. Inform new faculty of the criteria for promotion and tenure and the weight given to each criterion at the time of hiring. The new faculty member should be aware from the beginning of his or her employment exactly what the department and the college expect in terms of performance and productivity. If publications are essential to tenure and good teaching is a necessary but not sufficient condition for tenure, such an expectation should be made clear to the new faculty member. If standards "tighten up" during the period of probation, the higher expectations should be communicated to faculty who will be judged using those heightened standards. In short, faculty should be "on notice" of how they will be evaluated.

2. Department chairs or other senior faculty should evaluate probationary faculty annually. Annual evaluations of probationary faculty are useful because they provide feedback to junior faculty about their performance; they also give the department an opportunity to assess the candidate's progress toward the tenure evaluation. Some departments evaluate probationary faculty against the criteria for tenure annually, requiring the faculty member to prepare an informal dossier each year similar to the eventual tenure materials. Such a procedure makes it clear to the probationary faculty member what the criteria are and how his or her record is viewed by the department (or at least its chair), and the review helps the faculty member develop a complete and well-documented tenure dossier. Such a series of annual dress rehearsals for the eventual tenure review provides the department with extensive documentation of the candidate's progress (or lack thereof) toward tenure, identifies weaknesses in the candidate's performance or productivity while there is still time to correct those weaknesses, and eliminates the surprise when a junior faculty member is denied tenure after receiving no negative feedback (or no feedback at all) from the department. Admittedly, annual reviews of untenured faculty are time-consuming for all involved. Furthermore, if these reviews are insufficiently rigorous, a department may find it difficult to deny tenure to a colleague it has permitted to coast through probation. If the candidate and the department take these annual reviews seriously, however, they can help a good faculty member improve or can help a department document why a marginal faculty member should be denied tenure.

3. The college should be very forthright about the evidence used to make an employment decision. Should the decision be challenged in court, the college may be required to provide the faculty plaintiff with the materials upon which the negative decision was based. The administration should make it very clear to peer evaluation groups, department chairs, and deans how letters from external reviewers, student evaluations, and other materials will be used to evaluate a faculty member. If a faculty member's unsatisfactory performance has been documented annually, as suggested above, such documentation may be sufficient to defend the college against alleged discrimination or some other illegal employment practice. If decision makers rely on letters from outside experts, the college may decide to provide the plaintiff with a list of the evaluators and a summary of their comments without identifying the author of each evaluation. Considerations of confidentiality for evaluators need to be balanced with the interests of faculty plaintiffs in obtaining evidence to prove their allegations (Lee 1982–83); such issues are complex and the outcome often depends upon the circumstances of each particular case [*Gray* v. *Board of Higher Education,* 692 F.2d 901 (2d Cir. 1982)].

Salary Decisions

Although decisions about salary often do not have the individual impact of decisions about promotion and tenure, a judicial finding of systemic discrimination in salaries could virtually bankrupt a college or university. The following suggestions should help colleges avoid such a cataclysmic event.

1. The college should review the salaries of its faculty, perhaps using regression analysis. Administrators should consider adjusting salaries that have been found to be significantly lower than the predicted salary indicated by the regression analysis; this adjustment should be made irrespective of gender or race [*Board of Regents, University of Nebraska* v. *Dawes,* 522 F.2d 380 (8th Cir. 1975), *cert. denied,* 96 S. Ct. 1112 (1976)].

2. The college should develop a set of written guidelines for setting initial salaries for new faculty, deciding regular salary increases, assuming such decisions are not fixed by contract or salary scale, upgrading salaries to keep pace with new entry salary levels, and determining merit increases, assuming no collective bargaining agreement prohibits merit pay. Faculty should be involved in the development of the procedures, even if the ultimate decision is the responsibility of the administration.

3. The criteria for deciding salary should be made clear to faculty, and if such criteria require documentation, a mechanism for collecting data should be developed. For example, if excellent teaching is a criterion for a higher-than-average salary increase, it is clearly in the college's interest to design a system that will permit excellent teaching to be identified and documented rather than relying on undocumented judgments of departments chairs or deans.

4. If "market factors" are used to set starting salaries or to determine salary increases, they should be supported with evidence. Decision makers can survey similar colleges to ascertain the going rate for a doctorate in chemistry or English literature. Mean salaries in an academic discipline can be used to justify a decision. Legitimate job offers, including the offered salary, from other institutions are neutral factors acceptable in determining salary.

The litigation involving academic salary discrimination has not made it impossible for administrators to recognize differences in effort, ability, or the value of a certain kind of expertise and training and to reward certain faculty with higher salaries. The cases do, however, require that these differences be documented and that they bear a rational relationship to the mission of the college or university. As with peer evaluations, the courts will generally uphold salary decisions based upon neutral criteria and justified by evidence.

Other Conditions of Employment

The requirements of Title VII and Title IX are similar with regard to recruitment, hiring, promotion, and compensation of college faculty. Following the suggestions outlined in this chapter should help a college avoid litigation under Titles VII and IX, the Age Discrimination in Employment

Act, and the Equal Pay Act. A few general suggestions as
to employment practices, apart from performance evaluation and salaries, are in order at this point.

*1. The makeup of the search committee should be
sensitive to both institutional concerns and affirmative
action needs.* Search committees for academics (faculty or
administrators) should be limited to academics and students. If the composition of the search committee is limited
to one race or either sex, a minority representative from
another department, or even from another institution,
could be invited to serve on the committee. Affirmative
action should be a major concern of search and recruitment, irrespective of the composition of the search committee.

*2. Search committees recruiting for faculty or adminis-
trative positions should take care that the criteria used to
select the candidate are clearly related to the duties of the
job as well as to the criteria against which the individual
will be evaluated.* Any discrepancies, such as the selection
of an individual whose qualifications do not match the job
description, should be documented *in writing* at the time
the individual is selected, and criteria used to evaluate the
individual's job performance may have to be modified
accordingly.

*3. Administrators should check the institution's fringe
benefit policies to make sure that differences in benefit
levels (e.g., annuity payments) are based strictly upon
actuarial considerations and not solely on the basis of
gender or age.* The Supreme Court has ruled that fringe
benefits may not vary according to the employee's gender;
administrators should ask their counsel to review fringe
benefit practices in light of recent and current litigation.
Policies on sick leave, leaves without pay, and maternity
leaves should also be evaluated against Title VII and Title
IX regulations.

*4. Although tenure can be separated from employment
if the employment contract specifies that* tenure *ends when
an employee reaches a certain age, the employee may not
be terminated solely on the basis of age until the individual
reaches the age of 70.* Conditions surrounding ADEA are
in considerable flux; it behooves colleges to design attract-
ive incentives for early retirement. Successful early
retirement packages have been developed recently in a

number of states. Administrators and their counsel should check state laws and administrative regulations, however, before instituting any creative contract buy-outs or other early retirement plans.

Staff Terminations under Financial Exigency
Litigation involving the termination of tenured faculty has uniformly supported the legality of dissolving tenure if the institution is faced with a provable financial crisis. Even if an institution's employment contract, faculty handbook, or other policy documents omit references to financial exigency as a justification for reductions of tenured faculty, courts tend to apply the AAUP guidelines as "industrial practice" and generally will permit tenured faculty to be laid off if the fiscal crisis is bona fide. The following suggestions are drawn from recent litigation over financial exigency.

1. Both public and private institutions should be able to demonstrate bona fide financial exigency if administrators provide each faculty member to be laid off with a reasonably adequate written statement of the basis for the initial decision to lay off personnel, a description of the manner in which the initial decision was made, the information and data upon which decision makers relied, and the opportunity to respond (Johnson v. Board of Regents 1974, p. 240). The information given to the faculty member should include a description of the nature of and causes behind the financial exigency, the decision makers involved, the information and data used, how they were gathered and evaluated, and how the decision to lay off the faculty member was reached. The affected faculty members should have an opportunity to meet with the president, academic vice-president, or other decision makers to discuss the basis for the decision.

2. Objective measures, such as enrollments, changes in disciplinary emphasis, and new accreditation requirements, do not trigger concerns about dismissal "for cause" and do not require formal due process proceedings. If the criteria used to reach decisions are based upon subjective evaluations of ability or performance, the layoff may be viewed as one for cause, thus requiring a full-scale due process hearing.

3. The institution can demonstrate good faith in decisions about termination by considering candidates for layoff for vacant faculty or administrative positions or by attempting to find them positions at other institutions.

4. Because the courts tend to scrutinize the validity of the college's claim of financial exigency, using financial exigency as a pretext for terminating troublesome faculty may not only be unsuccessful but may also prejudice a college's future attempts to prove that a bona fide fiscal crisis exists. Such a mechanism for reducing staff should be used only when no alternative exists; otherwise, judicial approval of such a defense may no longer be available.

A Final Caution

It is not possible to anticipate every employment situation covered by the laws and judicial opinions reviewed in this report. Much flexibility still exists in employment decision making, and it is nearly impossible to predict the outcome of a particular case before a particular judge in federal or state court.

But administrators and their counsel can learn from the experiences of their colleagues. Just as one should consult his physician before changing his diet or program of exercise, administrators should consult counsel before modifying personnel policies and procedures; collective bargaining agreements, faculty bylaws, or other quasi-contractual policy documents may regulate the types of changes to be made and the means by which the changes are made. The suggestions in this chapter are culled from judicial precedent and statutory interpretation. Faculty and administrators, working cooperatively, should be able to expand and improve on them.

BIBLIOGRAPHY

The ERIC Clearinghouse on Higher Education abstracts and indexes the current literature on higher education for the National Institute of Education's monthly bibliographic journal *Resources in Education*. Most of these publications are available through the ERIC Document Reproduction Service (EDRS). For publications cited in this bibliography that are available from EDRS, ordering number and price are included. Readers who wish to order a publication should write to the ERIC Document Reproduction Service, P.O. Box 190, Arlington, Virginia 22210. When ordering, please specify the document number. Documents are available as noted in microfiche (MF) and paper copy (PC). Since prices are subject to change it is advisable to check the latest issue of *Resources in Education* for current cost based on the number of pages in the publication.

Cases and Statutes

Academic employment cases—general

AAUP v. *Bloomfield College*, 346 A.2d 615 (N.J. 1975).

Acosta v. *University of the District of Columbia*, 528 F. Supp. 1215 (D.D.C. 1981).

Bignall v. *North Idaho College*, 538 F.2d 243 (9th Cir. 1976).

Board of Regents v. *Roth*, 408 U.S. 564 (1972).

Chitwood v. *Feaster*, 468 F.2d 359 (4th Cir. 1972).

Chung v. *Park*, 514 F.2d 382 (3d Cir. 1975).

Clark v. *Holmes*, 474 F.2d 928 (7th Cir. 1972).

Davis v. *Oregon State University*, 591 F.2d 493 (9th Cir. 1978).

Duke v. *North Texas State University*, 469 F.2d 829 (5th Cir. 1972).

Endress v. *Brookdale Community College*, 364 A.2d 1080 (N.J. Super., A.D., 1976).

Faro v. *New York University*, 502 F.2d 1229 (2d Cir. 1974).

Ferguson v. *Thomas*, 430 F.2d 852 (5th Cir. 1970).

In re: Dinnan, 661 F.2d 426 (11th Cir. 1981), *cert. denied*, 102 S. Ct. 2904 (1982).

Kunda v. *Muhlenberg College*, 621 F.2d 532 (3d Cir. 1980).

Levitt v. *Board of Trustees of Nebraska State Colleges*, 376 F. Supp. 945 (D. Neb. 1974).

Lynn v. *Regents of the University of California*, 656 F.2d 1337 (9th Cir. 1981), *cert. denied*, _____ U.S. _____ (1982).

Marshall v. *Georgia Southwestern College*, 489 F. Supp. 1322 (M.D. Ga. 1980).

Mecklenberg v. *Board of Regents of Montana State University*, 13 Empl. Prac. Dec. ¶11,438 (D. Mont. 1976).

Papadopoulos v. *Oregon State Board of Higher Education*, 511 P.2d 854 (Ore. 1973), *cert. denied*, 417 U.S. 919 (1974).

Perry v. *Sinderman*, 408 U.S. 593 (1972).

Poterma v. *Ping*, 462 F. Supp. 328 (S.D. Ohio 1978).

Sweezy v. *New Hampshire*, 354 U.S. 234 (1957).

Trustees of Dartmouth College v. *Woodward*, 4 Wheat. (U.S.) 518 (1819).

Wellner v. *Minnesota State Junior College Board*, 487 F.2d 153 (8th Cir. 1973).

Discrimination in academic employment decisions

Acosta v. *University of the District of Columbia*, 528 F. Supp. 1215 (D.D.C. 1981).

Board of Regents v. *Bakke*, 438 U.S. 265 (1978).

Board of Regents, University of Nebraska v. *Dawes*, 522 F.2d 380 (8th Cir. 1975), *cert. denied*, 96 S. Ct. 1112 (1976).

Campbell v. *Ramsey*, 22 Fair Empl. Prac. Cases 83 (E.D. Ark. 1980).

Christensen v. *State of Iowa*, 563 F.2d 353 (8th Cir. 1977).

Clark v. *Whiting*, 607 F.2d 634 (4th Cir. 1979).

Cohen v. *Community College of Philadelphia*, 484 F. Supp. 411 (E.D. Pa. 1980).

County of Washington v. *Gunther*, 452 U.S. 161 (1981).

Craig v. *Alabama State University*, 451 F. Supp. 1207 (M.D. Ala. 1978).

Cramer v. *Virginia Commonwealth University*, 415 F. Supp. 673 (D. Va. 1976).

Cussler v. *University of Maryland*, 430 F. Supp. 602 (D. Md. 1977).

Davis v. *Weidner*, 596 F.2d 726 (7th Cir. 1979).

EEOC v. *Tufts*, 421 F. Supp. 152 (D. Mass. 1975).

EEOC v. *University of New Mexico*, 504 F.2d 1296 (10th Cir. 1974).

EEOC v. *University of Notre Dame du Lac*, 551 F. Supp. 737 (7th Cir. 1982).

Fair Labor Standards Act, 29 U.S.C. §201 (1978).

Faro v. *New York University*, 502 F.2d 1229 (2d Cir. 1974).

Fisher v. *Dillard*, 26 Fair Empl. Prac. Cases 184 (E.D. La. 1980).

Gray v. *Board of Higher Education*, 692 F.2d 901 (2d Cir. 1982).

Green v. *Board of Regents*, 474 F.2d 594 (5th Cir. 1973).

Griggs v. *Duke Power Co.*, 401 U.S. 424 (1971).

Hill v. *Nettleton*, 455 F. Supp. 514 (D. Col. 1978).

In re: Dinnan, 661 F.2d 426 (11th Cir. 1981), *cert. denied*, 102 S. Ct. 2904 (1982).

Jawa v. *Fayetteville State University*, 426 F. Supp. 218 (E.D.N.C. 1976).

Jepsen v. *Florida Board of Regents*, 610 F.2d 1379 (5th Cir. 1980).

Johnson v. *University of Pittsburgh*, 435 F. Supp. 1328 (W.D. Pa. 1977).

Keddie v. *Pennsylvania State University*, 412 F. Supp. 1264 (M.D. Pa. 1976).

Keyes v. *Lenoir Rhyne College*, 15 Fair Empl. Prac. Cases 914 (W.D.N.C. 1976), *aff'd*, 552 F.2d 579 (4th Cir. 1977), *cert. denied*, 434 U.S. 904 (1977).

Kunda v. *Muhlenberg College*, 621 F.2d 532 (3d Cir. 1980).

Labat v. *Board of Higher Education*, 401 F. Supp. 753 (S.D.N.Y. 1975).

LaBorde v. *Regents, University of California*, 495 F. Supp. 1067 (C.D. Cal. 1980), *aff'd*, 674 F.2d 1323 (9th Cir. 1982).

Lieberman v. *Gant*, 474 F. Supp. 848 (D. Conn. 1979), *aff'd*, 630 F.2d 60 (2d Cir. 1980).

Lincoln v. *Board of Regents of the University System of Georgia*, 697 F.2d 928 (11th Cir. 1983).

Lynn v. *Regents of the University of California*, 656 F.2d 1337 (9th Cir. 1981), *cert. denied*, _____ U.S. _____ (1982).

McKillop v. *Regents, University of California*, 386 F. Supp. 1270 (N.D. Cal. 1975).

Marshall v. *Georgia Southwestern College*, 489 F. Supp. 1322 (M.D. Ga. 1980).

Mecklenberg v. *Board of Regents of Montana State University*, 13 Empl. Prac. Dec. ¶11,438 (D. Mont. 1976).

Megill v. *Board of Regents*, 541 F.2d 1073 (5th Cir. 1976).

Melani v. *Board of Higher Education, City of New York*, 561 F. Supp. 769 (S.D.N.Y. 1983).

Molthan v. *Temple University*, 442 F. Supp. 448 (E.D. Pa. 1977).

Ollman v. *Toll*, 518 F. Supp. 1196 (D. Md. 1981), *aff'd*, _____ F.2d _____ (4th Cir. 1983).

Perham v. *Ladd*, 436 F. Supp. 1101 (N.D. Ill. E.D., 1977).

Peters v. *Middlebury College*, 409 F. Supp. 857 (D. Vt. 1976).

Powell v. *Syracuse University*, 580 F.2d 1150 (2d Cir. 1978).

Rajender v. *University of Minnesota*, 20 Empl. Prac. Dec. ¶30,225 (D. Minn. 1979).

Scott v. *University of Delaware*, 20 Empl. Prac. Dec. ¶30,027 (3d Cir. 1979).

§1981 of the Civil Rights Act, 42 U.S.C. §1981 (1978).

Shipley v. *Fisk University*, 8 Empl. Prac. Dec. ¶9538 (M.D. Tenn. 1973).

Smith v. *University of North Carolina*, 632 F.2d 316 (4th Cir. 1980).

Sobel v. *Yeshiva University*, 566 F. Supp. 1166 (S.D.N.Y. 1983).

Spieldoch v. *Maryville College*, 13 Fair Empl. Prac. Cases 660 (E.D. Mo. 1975).

Sweeney v. *Board of Trustees of Keene State College*, 439 U.S. 24 (1978). (*Sweeney I*).

Sweeney v. *Board of Trustees of Keene State College*, 604 F.2d 106 (1st Cir. 1979), *cert. denied*, 444 U.S. 1045 (1980). (*Sweeney II*).

Texas Department of Community Affairs v. *Burdine*, 101 S. Ct. 1089 (1981).

Title VII of the Civil Rights Act of 1964, 42 U.S.C §2000e *et seq.* (1978).

Title IX of the Education Amendments of 1972, 20 U.S.C. §1681 *et seq.* (1978).

Van de Vate v. *Bolling*, 379 F. Supp. 925 (E.D. Tenn. N.D., 1974).

Whiting v. *Jackson State*, 616 F.2d 116 (5th Cir. 1980).

Wilkens v. *University of Houston*, 654 F.2d 388 (5th Cir. 1981).

Title IX and employment

Bennett v. *West Texas State University*, 525 F. Supp. 77 (N.D. Tex. 1981).

Bob Jones University v. *Johnson*, 396 F. Supp. 597 (D.S.C. 1974), *aff'd mem.*, 529 F.2d 514 (4th Cir. 1975).

Cannon v. *the University of Chicago*, 441 U.S. 677 (1979). (*Cannon I*).

Cannon v. *the University of Chicago*, 648 F.2d 1104 (7th Cir. 1981), *cert. denied*, 454 U.S. 811 (1981). (*Cannon II*).

Dougherty County School System v. *Harris*, 622 F.2d 735 (5th Cir. 1980), *vacated sub nom Bell* v. *Dougherty County School System*, 102 S. Ct. 2264 (1982).

Grove City College v. *Bell*, 687 F.2d 684 (3d Cir. 1982), *cert. granted*, 51 U.S.L.W. 3611 (Feb. 22, 1983).

Guardian Association of New York City Police Department v. *Civil Service Commission of the City of New York*, 633 F.2d 233 (2d Cir. 1980), *cert. granted*, 51 U.S.L.W. 3547 (Jan. 11, 1982).

Haffer v. *Temple University*, 688 F.2d 14 (3d Cir. 1982).

Junior College District of St. Louis v. *Califano*, 597 F.2d 424 (1st Cir. 1979), *cert. denied*, 444 U.S. 972 (1979).

Lieberman v. *University of Chicago*, 660 F.2d 1185 (7th Cir. 1981), *cert. denied*, 102 S. Ct. 1993 (1982).

North Haven Board of Education v. *Bell*, 456 U.S. 512 (1982).

North Haven Board of Education v. *Hufstedler*, 629 F.2d 773 (2d Cir. 1980), *cert. granted* (see *North Haven* v. *Bell*).

Romeo Community Schools v. *HEW*, 600 F.2d 581 (6th Cir. 1979), *cert. denied*, 444 U.S. 972 (1979).

Seattle University v. *HEW*, 621 F.2d 992 (9th Cir. 1980), *vacated sub nom United States Department of Education* v. *Seattle University*, 102 S. Ct. 2264 (1982).

University of Richmond v. *Bell*, 543 F. Supp. 321 (E.D. Va. 1982).

University of Toledo v. *HEW*, 464 F. Supp. 693 (N.D. Ohio 1979).

Financial exigency and mandatory retirement

AAUP v. *Bloomfield College*, 136 N.J. Super 442, 346 A.2d 615 (App. Div. 1975).

Arizona Governing Committee v. *Norris*, 103 S. Ct. 3492 (1983).

Arnett v. *Kennedy*, 416 U.S. 134 (1974).

Bignall v. *North Idaho College*, 538 F.2d 243 (9th Cir. 1976).

Board of Regents v. *Roth*, 408 U.S. 564 (1972).

Brenna v. *Southern Colorado State College*, 589 F.2d 475 (10th Cir. 1978).

Browzin v. *Catholic University of America*, 527 F.2d 843 (D.C. Cir. 1975).

Council of New Jersey State College Locals, NJSFT-AFT/AFL-CIO v. *State Board of Higher Education*, 91 N.J. 18, 449 A.2d 1244 (1982).

Drans v. *Providence College*, 383 A.2d 1033 (R.I. 1978).

EEOC v. *Wyoming*, 514 F. Supp. 595 (D. Wyo. 1981), 51 U.S.L.W. 4219 (March 2, 1983).

Grany v. *Board of Regents of the University of Wisconsin System*, 92 Wisc. 2d 745, 286 N.W. 2d 138 (1979).

Hodel v. *Virginia Surface Mining and Reclamation Assn., Inc.*, 452 U.S. 264 (1981).

Jiminez v. *Almondovar*, 650 F.2d 363 (1st Cir. 1981).

Johnson v. *Board of Regents of the University of Wisconsin System*, 377 F. Supp. 227 (W.D. Wisc. 1974), *aff'd*, 510 F.2d 975 (7th Cir. 1975).

Karr v. *the Board of Trustees of Michigan State University*, 325 N.W. 2d 605 (Mich. App. 1982).

Klein v. *the Board of Higher Education of the City of New York*, 434 F. Supp. 1113 (S.D.N.Y. 1977).

Krotkoff v. *Goucher College*, 585 F.2d 675 (4th Cir. 1978).

Leftwich v. *Harris Stowe State College*, 540 F. Supp. 37 (E.D. Mo. 1982).

Levine v. *Fairleigh Dickinson University,* 646 F.2d 825 (3d Cir. 1981).

Levitt v. *Board of Trustees of Nebraska State College,* 376 F. Supp. 945 (1974).

Lumpert v. *University of Dubuque,* 225 N.W. 2d (Iowa Ct. of Appeals no. 2-57568, April 14, 1977).

McCroan v. *Bailey,* 543 F. Supp. 1201 (S.D. Ga. 1982).

National League of Cities v. *Usery,* 426 U.S. 833 (1976).

Perry v. *Sinderman,* 408 U.S. 593 (1972).

Sanders v. *Duke University,* 538 F. Supp. 1143 (M.D.N.C. 1982).

Scheuer v. *Creighton University,* 199 Neb. 618, 260 N.W. 2d 595 (1977).

Steinmetz v. *Board of Trustees of Community College District no. 529,* 68 Ill. App. 3d 83, 385 N.W. 2d 745 (1979).

Wood v. *Strickland,* 420 U.S. 308 (1975).

Books and Periodicals

Academe. 1982. "Economic Status of the Profession, 1981–82" 68:1–84.

Adams, John F., and Hall, John W. 1976. "Risk Management Concepts and Practices." *Journal of College and University Law* 3:127–253.

Aiken, Ray J. 1976. "Legal Liabilities in Higher Education: Their Scope and Management." *Journal of College and University Law* 3:254–448.

Altbach, Philip G., and Berdahl, Robert D., eds. 1981. *Higher Education in American Society.* Buffalo: Prometheus Books.

American Association of University Professors. 1974. "On Institutional Problems Resulting from Financial Exigencies: Some Operating Guidelines." *AAUP Bulletin* 60:270.

———. 1977. *AAUP Policy Documents and Reports.* Washington, D.C.: AAUP. ED 136 646. 105 pp. MF–$1.17; PC–$11.12.

Association of American Colleges. 1981a. *On Campus with Women* No. 30. Project on the Status and Education of Women. ED 205 139. 17 pp. MF–$1.17; PC–$3.74.

———. 1981b. *On Campus with Women* No. 32. Project on the Status and Education of Women. ED 213 299. 14 pp. MF–$1.17; PC–$3.74.

Balch, Pamela M. 1980. *Faculty Evaluation in Higher Education: A Review of Court Cases and Implications for the 1980's.* ED 187 285. 50 pp. MF–$1.17; PC–$5.49.

Baldridge, J.V.; Curtis, D. V.; Ecker, G.; and Riley, G. L. 1978. *Policy Making and Effective Leadership.* San Francisco: Jossey-Bass.

Bergman, Jerry. 1980. "Peer Evaluation of University Faculty." *College Student Journal* 14:1–21.

Black's Law Dictionary. 1979. 5th ed. St. Paul: West Publishing.

Blynn, Kathy. 1981. "Title IX of the Education Amendments of 1972: Does It Protect Employees of Educational Institutions?" *Brooklyn Law Review* 47:1075–1104.

Bolger, Michael T., and Wilmoth, David D. 1982. "Dismissal of Tenured Faculty Members for Financial Exigencies." *Marquette Law Review* 65:347–65.

Bompey, Stuart H. 1979. "1979 Update: Cases and Issues in Age Discrimination." *Journal of College and University Law* 6:195–230.

————. 1981. "Decoupling Tenure and Employment under the 1978 Amendments to the Age Discrimination in Employment Act." *Journal of College and University Law* 8:427–32.

Brooklyn Law Review. 1981. "Title IX of the Education Amendments of 1972: Does It Protect Employees of Educational Institutions?" 47:1075–1104.

Brown, R. C. 1977. "Tenure Rights in Contractual and Constitutional Context." *Journal of Law and Education* 6:279–318.

California Law Review. 1981. "Note: Preventing Unnecessary Intrusions on University Autonomy: A Proposed Academic Freedom Privilege" 69:1538–68.

Carnegie Council on Policy Studies in Higher Education. 1980. *Three Thousand Futures*. San Francisco: Jossey-Bass. ED 183 076. 175 pp. MF–$1.17; PC not available EDRS.

Centra, John. 1980. *Determining Faculty Effectiveness*. San Francisco: Jossey-Bass.

Chait, Richard P., and Ford, Andrew F. 1982. *Beyond Traditional Tenure*. San Francisco: Jossey-Bass.

Chronicle of Higher Education. 1 September 1982a. "Colleges Ask Congress to Defeat Bills Ending Mandatory Retirement" 25:23.

————. 29 September 1982b. "Excerpts from AAUP Report on 'Uncapping' Retirement Age" 25:28.

————. 13 October 1982c. "The Supreme Court and Faculty Rights: Retirement, Sex Bias, and Tenure" 25:25–26.

————. 27 October 1982d. "Colorado State University Panel Proposes Program Cuts" 25:3.

————. 1 December 1982e. "On Oregon's Campuses the Refrain Is 'We Can't Cut Anything More' " 25:6.

Clark, Donald L. 1977. "Discrimination Suits: A Unique Settlement." *Educational Record* 58:233–40.

Code of Federal Regulations. "Nondiscrimination on the Basis of Sex in Activities Receiving or Benefiting from Federal Financial Assistance." 34 C.F.R. §§106.1 *et seq.*

Drucker, Peter M. 1980. *Managing in Turbulent Times*. New York: Harper & Row.

Duerr, C. A. 1 March 1980. "Termination of Tenured Faculty." Unpublished outline prepared for the Mid-winter Continuing Legal Education Workshop sponsored by the National Association of College and University Attorneys by Jackson, Lamb, and Duerr. Ypsilanti, Michigan.

Edwards, Harry T., and Nordin, Virginia Davis. 1979. *Higher Education and the Law*. Cambridge: Harvard University Press.

Finkelstein, Michael O. 1980. "The Judicial Reception of Multiple Regression Studies in Race and Sex Discrimination Cases." *Columbia Law Review* 80:737–54.

Fisher, Franklin M. 1980. "Multiple Regression in Legal Proceedings." *Columbia Law Review* 80:702–36.

Flygare, Thomas J. 1980–81. "*Board of Trustees of Keene State College* v. *Sweeney:* Implications for the Future of Peer Review in Faculty Personnel Decisions." *Journal of College and University Law* 7:100–110.

Foster, Stephen. November 1981. "NACUBO Report: Mandatory Retirement." *Business Officer* 15(5):16–18.

Furniss, Todd W., and Gardner, David P. 1979. *Higher Education and Government*. Washington, D.C.: American Council on Education.

Gaal, John, and Dibrenao, Louis P. 1980. "The Legality and Requirements of HEW's Proposed Policy Interpretation of Title IX and Intercollegiate Athletics." *Journal of College and University Law* 6:161–94.

Gray, John A. 1980. "Higher Education Litigation: Financial Exigency." *University of San Francisco Law Review* 14:375–402.

———. 1981. "Legal Restraints on Faculty Cutbacks." In *Challenges of Retrenchment,* edited by James F. Mingle. San Francisco: Jossey-Bass.

Green, Debra H. 1980–81. "An Application of the Equal Pay Act to Higher Education." *Journal of College and University Law* 8:203–18.

Greenfield, Ester. 1977. "From Equal to Equivalent Pay: Salary Discrimination in Academia." *Journal of Law and Education* 6:41–62.

Guthrie, Claire R. 29 September 1982. "Can Tenure Be 'Decoupled' from Retirement? An Analysis of the Law." *Chronicle of Higher Education* 25:28.

Hample, S. R., ed. 1981. *Coping with Faculty Reduction*. New Directions for Institutional Research No. 30. San Francisco: Jossey-Bass.

Hendrickson, Robert M. 1981. "Legal Aspects of Faculty Reduction." In *Coping with Faculty Reduction,* edited by Stephen R. Hample. New Directions for Institutional Research No. 30. San Francisco: Jossey-Bass.

———. 1982. "Faculty Issues in the Eighties." *Phi Delta Kappan* 64:338–41.

Hendrickson, Robert M., and Mangum, Ronald Scott. 1977. *Governing Board and Administrator Liability.* AAHE-ERIC/ Higher Education Report No. 9. Washington, D.C.: American Association for Higher Education. ED 148 256. 72 pp. MF–$1.17; PC–$7.24.

Higher Education Daily. 1 November 1982. "Michigan State Faculty Protest Forced Layoffs" 10:4.

Hobbs, Walter C., ed. 1978. *Government Regulation of Higher Education.* Cambridge, Mass.: Ballinger Publishing Co.

———. 1981. "The Courts." In *Higher Education in American Society,* edited by Philip G. Altbach and Robert O. Berdahl. Buffalo: Prometheus Books.

———, ed. 1982. *Understanding Academic Law.* New Directions for Institutional Advancement No. 16. San Francisco: Jossey-Bass.

Holloway, J. P. 1980. "Termination of Faculty due to Financial Exigency." *Journal of the College and University Personnel Association* 31:84–94.

Iowa Law Review. 1976. "Financial Exigency as Cause for Termination of Tenured Faculty in Private Postsecondary Educational Institutions" 62:481–521.

Johnson, George, and Stafford, Frank. 1974. "The Earnings and Promotion of Women Faculty." *American Economic Review* 64:888–903.

Kaplin, William A. 1978. *The Law of Higher Education.* San Francisco: Jossey-Bass.

———. 1980. *The Law of Higher Education 1980.* San Francisco: Jossey-Bass.

Koch, James V. 1982. "Salary Equity Issues in Higher Education: Where Do We Stand?" *AAHE Bulletin* 35(2):7–14.

LaNoue, George R. March 1982. "Judicial Responses to Academic Salary Discrimination." Paper presented at the annual conference of the Association for the Study of Higher Education, Washington, D.C.

Lee, Barbara A. 1982–83. "Balancing Confidentiality and Disclosure in Faculty Peer Review." *Journal of College and University Law* 9:279–314.

Lester, Richard A. 1980. *Reasoning about Discrimination.* Princeton: Princeton University Press.

Louisell, D., and Mueller, C. 1978. *Federal Evidence*. 2:§§228–29.

McFadden, Robert D. 19 March 1983. "U.S. Court Rules against City U. in Sex-Bias Suit." *New York Times*.

Magarrell, Jack. 15 September 1982. "Fall Enrollment May Set Record Despite Economy, High Tuition." *Chronicle of Higher Education* 25:11.

Marwell, Gerald; Rosenfeld, Rachel; and Spilerman, Seymour. 1979. "Geographic Constraints on Women's Careers in Academia." *Science* 205:1225–31.

Michigan Law Review. 1980. "Title VI, Title IX, and the Private University: Defining 'Recipient' and 'Program or Part Thereof' " 78:608–25.

Mingle, James F., ed. 1981. *Challenges of Retrenchment*. San Francisco: Jossey-Bass.

Mitzman, Barry. 10 November 1982. "University of Washington Plans to Drop 24 Degree Programs." *Chronicle of Higher Education* 25:3.

Mix, Marjorie C. 1978. *Tenure and Termination in Financial Exigency*. AAHE-ERIC/Higher Education Report No. 3. Washington, D.C.: American Association for Higher Education. ED 152 222. 37 pp. MF–$1.17; PC–$5.49.

Mortimer, Kenneth, and McConnell, T. R. 1978. *Sharing Authority Effectively*. San Francisco: Jossey-Bass.

Murphy, Dorothy E. 1981. "Title IX: An Alternative Remedy for Sex-Based Employment Discrimination for the Academic Employee?" *St. John's Law Review* 55:329–45.

Nelson, Bruce A., and Ward, Richard W. 1980. "Burden of Proof under Employment Discrimination Legislation." *Journal of College and University Law* 6:301-16.

North Carolina Law Review. 1982. "Civil Rights—Academic Freedom, Secrecy, and Subjectivity as Obstacles to Proving a Title VII Sex Discrimination Suit in Academia" 60:438–50.

Olswang, Steven G. 1982–83. "Planning the Unthinkable: Issues in Institutional Reorganization and Faculty Reductions." *Journal of College and University Law* 9:431–49.

Olswang, Steven G.; Cole, Elsa K.; and Wilson, James B. 1982. "Program Elimination, Financial Emergency, and Student Rights." *Journal of College and University Law* 9:163–75.

Pezzullo, Thomas R., and Brittingham, Barbara E. 1979. *Salary Equity: Detecting Sex Bias in Salary among College and University Professors*. Lexington, Mass.: D.C. Heath–Lexington.

Runyon, John R. 1980. "Employment Decision Making in Educational Institutions." *Wayne Law Review* 26:955–1018.

Salomone, Rosemary C. 1979. "*North Haven* and *Dougherty:* Narrowing the Scope of Title IX." *Journal of Law and Education* 10:191–206.

———. 1980. "Title IX and Employment Discrimination: A Wrong in Search of a Remedy." *Journal of Law and Education* 9:433–45.

School Law Newsletter. 1978. "Financial Exigency and Reduction-in-Force" 7:287–93.

Scully, Malcolm G. 6 October 1982. "Possible Faculty Shortage in 1990s Worries Today's Academic Leaders." *Chronicle of Higher Education* 25:1.

Stadtman, Verne A. 1980. *Academic Adaptations.* San Francisco: Jossey-Bass.

University of Pennsylvania Law Review. 1980. "Eliminating Sex Discrimination in Educational Institutions: Does Title IX Reach Employment?" 129:417–51.

Van Gieson, Nan, and Zirkel, Perry A. 1981. "Fiscal Exitgency." *Educational Record* 62:75–77.

Vladeck, Judith P., and Young, Margaret M. 1978. "Sex Discrimination in Higher Education: It's Not Academic." *Women's Rights Law Reporter* 4:59–78.

Waintroob, Andrea R. 1979–80. "The Developing Law of Equal Employment Opportunity at the White Collar and Professional Level." *William and Mary Law Review* 21:45–119.

Washington University Law Quarterly. 1982. "Tenth Amendment Protects State Mandatory Retirement Policy against Federal Age Discrimination in Employment Act" 60:687–703.

Weeks, Kent M. 1980. "When Financial Exigency Justifies Dismissal." *AGB Reports* 22:35–40.

Wehrwein, Auston C. 9 February 1981. "Sex-Bias Claims Filed in Minnesota." *Chronicle of Higher Education* 21:10.

Yurko, Richard J. 1980. "Judicial Recognition of Academic Collective Interests: A New Approach to Faculty Title VII Litigation." *Boston University Law Review* 60:473–541.

ASHE-ERIC HIGHER EDUCATION
RESEARCH REPORTS

Starting in 1983 the Association for the Study of Higher Education assumed co-sponsorship of the Higher Education Research Reports with the ERIC Clearinghouse on Higher Education. For the previous 11 years ERIC and the American Association for Higher Education prepared and published the reports.

Each report is the definitive analysis of a tough higher education problem, based on a thorough research of pertinent literature and institutional experiences. Report topics, identified by a national survey, are written by noted practitioners and scholars with prepublication manuscript reviews by experts.

Ten monographs in the ASHE-ERIC/Higher Education Research Report series are published each year, available individually or by subscription. Subscription to 10 issues is $50 regular; $35 for members of AERA, AAHE, and AIR; $30 for members of ASHE. (Add $7.50 outside U.S.)

Prices for single copies, including 4th class postage and handling, are $6.50 regular and $5.00 for members of AERA, AAHE, AIR, and ASHE. If faster first-class postage is desired for U.S. and Canadian orders, for each publication ordered add $.60; for overseas, add $4.50. For VISA and MasterCard payments, give card number, expiration date, and signature. Orders under $25 must be prepaid. Bulk discounts are available on orders of 10 or more of a single title. Order from the Publications Department, Association for the Study of Higher Education, One Dupont Circle, Suite 630, Washington, D.C. 20036. (202) 296-2597. Write for a complete list of Higher Education Research Reports and other ASHE and ERIC publications.

1981 Higher Education Research Reports

1. Minority Access to Higher Education
   Jean L. Preer

2. Institutional Advancement Strategies in Hard Times
   Michael D. Richards and Gerald Sherratt

3. Functional Literacy in the College Setting
   Richard C. Richardson, Jr., Kathryn J. Martens, and Elizabeth C. Fisk

4. Indices of Quality in the Undergraduate Experience
   George D. Kuh

5. Marketing in Higher Education
   Stanley M. Grabowski

6. Computer Literacy in Higher Education
   Francis E. Masat

7. Financial Analysis for Academic Units
   Donald L. Walters

8. Assessing the Impact of Faculty Collective Bargaining
   J. Victor Baldridge, Frank R. Kemerer, and Associates

9. Strategic Planning, Management, and Decision Making
   Robert G. Cope

10. Organizational Communication in Higher Education
    Robert D. Gratz and Philip J. Salem

1982 Higher Education Research Reports

1. Rating College Teaching: Criterion Studies of Student
   Evaluation-of-Instruction Instruments
   Sidney E. Benton

2. Faculty Evaluation: The Use of Explicit Criteria for
   Promotion, Retention, and Tenure
   Neal Whitman and Elaine Weiss

3. The Enrollment Crisis: Factors, Actors, and Impacts
   *J. Victor Baldridge, Frank R. Kemerer, and Kenneth C.
   Green*

4. Improving Instruction: Issues and Alternatives for Higher
   Education
   Charles C. Cole, Jr.

5. Planning for Program Discontinuance: From Default to
   Design
   Gerlinda S. Melchiori

6. State Planning, Budgeting, and Accountability: Approaches
   for Higher Education
   Carol E. Floyd

7. The Process of Change in Higher Education Institutions
   Robert C. Nordvall

8. Information Systems and Technological Decisions: A Guide
   for Non-Technical Administrators
   Robert L. Bailey

9. Government Support for Minority Participation in Higher
   Education
   Kenneth C. Green

10. The Department Chair: Professional Development and Role
    Conflict
    David B. Booth

1983 Higher Education Research Reports

1. The Path to Excellence: Quality Assurance in Higher
   Education
   *Laurence R. Marcus, Anita O. Leone, and Edward D.
   Goldberg*